SECOND EDITION

Disclaimers *in* Estate Planning

CHRISTOPHER P. CLINE

ABA SECTION OF REAL PROPERTY | TRUST & ESTATE LAW

ABA
Defending Liberty
Pursuing Justice

Cover design by Elmarie Jara.

Printed in the United States of America.

16 15 14 13 12 5 4 3 2 1

Library of Congress Cataloging-in-Publication Data

Cline, Christopher P., 1960–
Disclaimers in estate planning / By Christopher P. Cline. — 2nd ed.
p. cm.
Includes bibliographical references and index.
ISBN 978-1-61438-429-8 (print : alk. paper) — ISBN 978-1-61438-430-4 (ebook)
1. Estate planning--United States. 2. Renunciation of inheritance—United States. I. Title.
KF750.Z9C59 2012
343.7305'3—dc23

2012008333

CONTENTS

About the Author

Christopher P. Cline is Wells Fargo Bank's Senior Regional Fiduciary Manager for Oregon and SW Washington. Before joining the financial services industry, he practiced estate planning law for over 15 years. Chris is a fellow of the American College of Trust and Estate Counsel. He has written *The Law of Trustee Investments* for the American Bar Association, five Tax Management Portfolios on various estate planning topics for the Bureau of National Affairs, chapters and one book on Oregon trust law, and numerous articles in national publications. He is a frequent speaker at various national estate planning seminars, and a past president of both the Portland Estate Planning Council and the Oregon State Bar's Estate Planning and Administration Section.

GENERAL 1

A. INTRODUCTION

The disclaimer is a strange creature. Though invented in England centuries ago (and referred to as waiver or renunciation),[1] the 1976 codification, in Section 2518 of the federal transfer tax law of disclaimer, popularized both the concept and the name "disclaimer." It is also conceptually strange, requiring the donee of a gift (either lifetime or testamentary) to reject it, so that the gift is never made.[2] Which begs the question, "Why would you refuse to accept a gift?"

There are two main reasons for doing so: first, the act of disclaiming, for federal transfer tax purposes, is not a transfer,[3] and therefore there is no tax on it from the disclaimant's perspective; and second, for state

---

1. *See, e.g.*, J. H. Martin, *Perspectives on Federal Disclaimer Legislation*, 46 U. CHI. L. REV. 316, fn. 2 (1979).

2. BROWN, PERSONAL PROPERTY, § 7.14 (3d ed. 1975).

3. § 2518(a). Regs. §§ 25.2518–1(b) and 25.2511–1(c)(2) ("a refusal to accept ownership does not constitute the making of a gift. . .").

law purposes (primarily debtor-creditor purposes), the disclaimant is deemed never to have possessed the disclaimed property.

The conceptual engine that drives the disclaimer is the "relation-back" concept: a disclaimer "relates back" to the original transfer of the interest disclaimed.[4] If Jane dies on July 1, 2008, leaving her estate to Bob and, within the time required, Bob makes a qualified disclaimer of that gift, the disclaimer is effective as of the date of Jane's death, not Bob's disclaimer. Jane's will or state law, or both, determine who takes her estate instead of Bob. Note that Bob has no say in where the estate assets go.

For example, Rev. Rul. 83–26[5] dealt with a husband's will that created a trust, all of the income of which was payable to the wife for life, with the remainder passing to the husband's children. After the husband died, his executor made a qualified terminable interest property (QTIP) election for the trust on the federal estate tax return. The wife later made a qualified disclaimer of her trust interest. The executor claimed that the QTIP election foreclosed the wife's disclaimer, and therefore the husband's estate was entitled to the marital deduction for the full value of the trust and the wife's subsequent disclaimer was actually a transfer of the QTIP property. However, the IRS ruled that, even though the executor's QTIP election had preceded the wife's disclaimer, the disclaimer related back to the date of the husband's death, so the disclaimed interest never passed to the wife and the transfer did not qualify for the QTIP election. The estate got no marital deduction, and the wife made no taxable transfer.

Disclaimers are governed by both state and federal law. Section 2518 introduced the term "qualified disclaimer" for federal transfer tax purposes, but it has little impact on the state law of disclaimers, and it does not apply to disclaimers made before 1977. For those earlier disclaimers (which are fairly rare), the tax law that applies involves a tangle of historical decisions, rulings, and regulations. Which means that the first thing a practitioner must do when determining whether a disclaimer is appropriate is to determine which federal law applies and how state law will affect it.

---

4. *See* § 2518(b)(2).
5. 1983–1 C.B. 234.

B. Overview of Federal Transfer Taxes

Section 2518 appears within Chapter 12 of the Internal Revenue Code, the gift tax chapter. However, the first sentence of Section 2518 makes it clear that this section provides the rules for disclaimer not only with respect to inter vivos gifts (Chapter 12) but also with respect to transfers of taxable estates (Chapter 11) and generation-skipping transfers (Chapter 13). Therefore, a very brief discussion of transfer taxes is appropriate. The transfer taxes (estate, gift, and generation-skipping transfer, or GST, taxes) are imposed on the gratuitous transfer of property,[6] based on a person's cumulative lifetime and testamentary transfers of property.[7] They are calculated on the fair market value of the property transferred.[8] The 2001 Tax Relief Act changed the tax rates, the unified credit exemption amounts, the deduction for qualified family-owned business interests, and the state death tax credit applicable in the interim before repeal.[9] Effective January 1, 2010, the estate and GST taxes were repealed. However, in December 2010, Congress (after much noise) reinstated the federal estate and GST taxes, with other significant changes, but only until December 31, 2012.[10]

The Tax Relief, Unemployment Reauthorization, and Job Creation Act of 2010, (the "2010 Act") allows for a $5 million exemption from estate, gift, and GST taxes and the "portability" of exemption between spouses, allowing a surviving spouse to use both his or her exemption as well as that of the predeceased spouse, for a total of up to $10 million of exemption.

6. *See* Regs. §§ 20.0–2(a), 25.0–1(b).
7. §§ 2001(b), 2502(a).
8. §§ 2032, 2032A, and 2512(b).
9. *See* Pub. L. No. 107-16, §§ 511, 521, 531, and 532.
10. *See, e.g.*, Beth S. Kaufman, *Finally, Legislation! Congress Kicks the Can Down the Road,* 38 Estate Planning 36 (June 2011).

C. Overview of Qualified Disclaimer

The overwhelming majority of disclaimers will be subject to the rules of Section 2518. The rare exception will be for the child who is a distributee of a pre-1977 decedent's estate or a beneficiary of a pre-1977 gift and who was a minor in 1976.[11] The regulations applicable to these early disclaimers generally permitted a disclaimer "within a reasonable time after knowledge of the existence of the transfer."[12] Arguably, the minority period for federal tax purposes[13] or local law minority period extends the "reasonable time." Further, the taker in default of a general power of appointment created under the will of a decedent who died before 1977 or under a pre-1977 inter vivos trust may still have years within which he or she can disclaim his or her interest because of the way in which the regulations determined the starting point for a disclaimer (however, if the power holder dies after 1976 and the power lasts until his or her death, the disclaimer is governed by Section 2518[14]).

The qualified disclaimer of Section 2518 must be made within nine months of the date of the decedent's death or the date of gift, or nine months after age 21 if the prospective disclaimant is under age 21 at that date.[15] A qualified disclaimer is an irrevocable and unqualified refusal to accept an interest, or undivided portion of an interest, in property,[16] which may include a power with respect to property.[17] The refusal must be in writing,[18] delivered to the transferor of the interest, his legal representative or the holder of the legal title to the property to which the interest relates, not

---

11. *But see* Ordway v. U.S., 89-1 USTC ¶ 13,802 (S.D. Fla. 1989), *rev'd*, 908 F.2d 890 (11th Cir. 1990), *cert. denied*, 501 U.S. 1261 (1991); Irvine v. U.S., 89-2 USTC ¶ 13,818 (D. Minn. 1989), *rev'd*, 936 F.2d 343 (8th Cir. 1991), *aff'd en banc*, 981 F.2d 991 (8th Cir. 1992), *rev'd*, 511 U.S. 224 (1994).

12. See Chapter 4.

13. *See, e.g.*, §§ 2503(c), 2518(b)(2)(B).

14. Regs. § 25.2518–2(c)(3).

15. § 2518(b)(2).

16. § 2518(b).

17. § 2518(c)(2).

18. § 2518(b)(1).

later than nine months after the date of the transfer creating the interest, or nine months after the disclaimant becomes 21.[19] The disclaimant must not have accepted the interest or any of its benefits.[20] As a result of the disclaimer, the interest must pass, without any direction on the part of the disclaimant, either to the spouse of the decedent or transferor[21] or to a person other than the disclaimant.[22] The details of these requirements will be discussed in future chapters.

---

19. § 2518(b)(2).
20. § 2518(b)(3).
21. § 2518(b)(4)(A). The spouse to whom the disclaimed interest passes can be the disclaimant. *See* PLR 200006052.
22. § 2518(b)(4)(B).

STATE DISCLAIMER LAWS 2

The starting point for any disclaimer is state law. Although the federal law issues tend to attract all the attention, if a disclaimer is not qualified for state law purposes, it will almost certainly fail for federal law purposes as well (although there are some minor exceptions, discussed below). State law governs how a disclaimer is made as well as what can and cannot be disclaimed.

Although each state's disclaimer law is different, they can be divided into two broad categories:

1. Those states that have adopted one or more of the Uniform Disclaimer Acts. These can be subdivided into three categories: (a) States that have adopted either or both the Uniform Disclaimer of Transfers by Will, Intestacy or Appointment Act and the Uniform Disclaimer of Transfers Under Nontestamentary Instruments Act, promulgated in 1978; (b) states that have adopted the 1978 Uniform Disclaimer of Property Interests Act; and (c) states that have adopted the new Uniform Disclaimer of Property Interests Act promulgated in 1999 and revised in 2002.

2. The many states (including several of the most populous) that have not adopted a uniform act, but rather have their own unique statutes. In this category, this book discusses the disclaimer statutes of California, Texas, and New York.

Although this book does not provide a complete survey of all state laws, the combination of these statutes provides a good starting point for discussing the issues common to all states.

A. BACKGROUND OF THE UNIFORM ACTS

Before discussing the particular laws of each state, it may be helpful to discuss briefly the somewhat confusing state of the Uniform Acts. To begin with, three Uniform Acts were promulgated in 1978. The Uniform Will, Intestacy and Appointment Act (the "Wills Act") and the Uniform Disclaimer of Transfers under Nontestamentary Instruments Act (the "Nontestamentary Act") were designed to be enacted together; the latter was designed simply as a companion piece to the Wills Act, covering inter vivos transfers. So, for example, the Nontestamentary Act covers disclaimers by beneficiaries under insurance policies, the "accretive portion derived through survivorship" of joint tenancy property and interests in joint bank accounts. Interestingly, although eleven states have adopted the Wills Act,[1] only four states have adopted the Nontestamentary Act.[2]

On the other hand, the 1978 Uniform Disclaimer of Property Interests Act (the "1978 Disclaimer Act") mirrors the provisions of the two separate disclaimer acts described above but, according to the Comment, "is designed for application in states where the codification system lends itself to a single Act."[3] However, the provisions in the 1978 Disclaimer Act are located in slightly different places than identical provisions in the other two.

1. Delaware, Florida, Idaho, Illinois, Kansas, Kentucky, Maine, Minnesota, Nebraska, New Jersey, and North Carolina.

2. Delaware, Kansas, Kentucky, and Maine.

3. Unless otherwise noted, all references in this section are to Uniform Laws Annotated, 1978 Uniform Disclaimer of Property Interests Act (West 2003).

Noting deficiencies in all three of the 1978 Acts, in 2002, the National Conference of Commissioners on Uniform State Laws approved a revised version of the Uniform Disclaimer of Property Interests Act (a prior version of this Uniform Act had been adopted in 1999). As of this writing, eight states have adopted it.[4]

Although the specific provisions of the four Acts are discussed in detail below, some general, more significant, changes should be discussed at the outset. The 1999 Disclaimer Act eliminates the specific time limit (nine months in the case of the 1978 Acts) on the making of any disclaimer. Instead, the only bar to a disclaimer "should be acceptance of the offer." The reason for this "decoupling" of the disclaimer statute from the time requirement under Section 2518 is that the nine-month time limit in the 1978 Acts did not correspond to the nine-month requirement in Section 2518, particularly in the case of the time limit for future interests.

Second, the 1999 Disclaimer Act abandons the relation-back concept "as a proxy for when a disclaimer becomes effective. Instead, by stating specifically when a disclaimer becomes effective and explicitly stating . . . that a disclaimer 'is not a transfer, assignment, or release,'" the Act clarifies the results of disclaiming property. Although the effect was intended to be the same under old and new law, it remains to be seen whether a court finds that this change has substantive significance.

Third, the 1999 Disclaimer Act creates rules for disclaimers that were not explicitly addressed in the 1978 Acts, including qualified disclaimers of jointly held property, disclaimers by trustees of property that otherwise would become part of a trust, disclaimers of powers of appointment and other powers *not* held in a fiduciary capacity, disclaimers by appointees and takers in default of exercise of a power of appointment, and disclaimers of powers held in a fiduciary capacity.

Fourth, the definition of the term *disclaimer*, defined as "the refusal to accept an interest in or power over property," expands previous definitions, according to the Comments. The added phrase referring to "power over property" broadens the scope of

4. Arkansas, Hawaii, Indiana, New Mexico, North Dakota, Oregon, Virginia, and West Virginia.

a disclaimer to include a right to control property, "whether it be cast in the form of a power of appointment or a fiduciary's management power over property or discretionary power of distribution over income or corpus." "Jointly held property" means property held by two or more people, all of whom "have concurrent interests and under which the last surviving holder is entitled to the whole of the property." This definition includes not only traditional joint tenancy but other property that is held with a right of survivorship. This might include a "joint bank account between parties who are not married to each other which, under the laws of many States, is owned by the parties in proportion to their deposits."

B. Who Can Disclaim?

Identifying who can disclaim (the "disclaimant") is obviously an important first step. The scope of potential disclaimants changes depending upon state law.

1. 1978 Uniform Acts

Section 1 of the Wills Act states that a person (or the representative of a deceased, incapacitated, or protected person) may disclaim. The disclaimant must be an "heir, next of kin, devisee, legatee, person succeeding to a disclaimed interest, beneficiary under a testamentary instrument or appointee under a power of appointment exercised by a testamentary instrument." The section also allows for successive disclaimers and "extends the right to disclaim to the representative of a decedent, as well as to a guardian or conservator."

The term *beneficiary* in the Nontestamentary Act is the same as that used in the Wills Act. The Comments to Section 1 of the Nontestamentary Act grant the right of disclaimer to a surviving joint tenant or the beneficiary under an insurance policy. According to the Comments, the position taken by the Nontestamentary Act is to "confer the right of disclaimer upon a surviving joint tenant and leave to the particular circumstances whether he may disclaim all of the interest or only the accretive part and the effect of knowledge of the existence of the tenancy, acceptance of benefits, and the like."

The 1978 Disclaimer Act, because of its comprehensive nature, provides a broader definition of the party that can disclaim: The right to disclaim is granted to "a person, or the representative of an incapacitated or protected person, to whom any property or interest therein evolves, by whatever means." At least two states that adopted this Act provide a more complete definition of who can disclaim.[5] Further, Section 2(d) of the 1978 Disclaimer Act provides that a "surviving joint tenant may disclaim a separate interest in any property or interest therein devolving to him by right of survivorship." A surviving joint tenant also "may disclaim the entire interest in any property or interest therein that is the subject of a joint tenancy devolving to him, if the joint tenancy was created by the act of a deceased joint tenant" and the survivor did not join in creating the joint tenancy. This provision also applies to tenancies by the entireties.

Interestingly, Section 1 of the 1978 Disclaimer Act does not refer to the representative of a deceased person among those persons who can disclaim property. Five states and the District of Columbia that have adopted the 1978 Disclaimer Act[6] have corrected this apparent oversight by including in their definitions of those who may be disclaimants the personal representatives of a deceased person's estate.

2. 1999 Uniform Act

Section 2 of the 1999 Disclaimer Act includes a new "definitions" section, different from the 1978 Acts. This new section defines "disclaimant" as the person who would have received the disclaimed property or power if the disclaimer had not been made. As the Comments point out, the disclaimant is "not necessarily the person making the disclaimer, who may be a guardian, custodian, or other fiduciary acting for the disclaimant, or the personal representative of the disclaimant's estate."

5. *See, e.g.*, Alabama and Delaware.
6. Alabama, Mississippi, New Hampshire, Vermont, and West Virginia.

3. California Law

California law also provides a broad definition of the party that can make a disclaimer. Under California Probate Code Section 262, a "beneficiary" is a person entitled, but for the person's disclaimer, to take an interest. A "disclaimant" is a beneficiary who executes a disclaimer on his or her own behalf or a person who executes a disclaimer on behalf of a beneficiary.[7] It also includes a conservator on behalf of a conservatee,[8] or representatives on behalf of minors or decedents.[9]

4. Texas Law

As with the California statute, Texas law provides that a broad class of parties can execute a disclaimer: It can be made by

> [a]ny person, or the guardian of an incapacitated person, the personal representative of a deceased person, or the guardian ad litem of an unborn or unascertained person, with prior court approval of the court having, or which would have, jurisdiction over such guardian, personal representative, or guardian ad litem, or any independent executor of a deceased person, without prior court approval, or an attorney in fact or agent appointed under a durable power of attorney authorizing disclaimers that is executed by a principal, who may be entitled to receive any property as a beneficiary and who intends to effect disclaimer irrevocably on or after September 1, 1977.[10]

5. New York Law

Under New York law, a renunciation (New York's term for *disclaimer*) may be made by the guardian of the property of an infant (with court authorization), the committee of an incompetent or the conservator of a conservatee (with court approval), a guardian

7. Cal. Prob. Code § 264 (West 2011).
8. Cal. Prob. Code § 276 (West 2011).
9. Cal. Prob. Code § 277 (West 2011).
10. Tex. Prob. Code § 37A (Vernon's 2011).

with authorization from the court, the personal representative of a decedent or an attorney-in-fact if authorized under a "duly executed power of attorney."[11] There are, however, additional requirements for certain renunciations by attorneys-in-fact.[12]

C. What Can Be Disclaimed?

1. 1978 Uniform Acts

In addition to disclaimers of outright gifts, the Wills Act allows disclaimers of "any survivorship interest in the community in a community property state," "partial interests in property (which includes not only a disclaimer of a fractional share but also a disclaimer of any limited interest or estate), administrative or investment powers, a power of appointment under a trust (which includes the possibility of reducing or limiting the power as to amount, objects or conditions,), or parts of the incidents of ownership of property (for example disclaiming all but a life estate in a devise of a fee interest)." The Nontestamentary Act adds little to the definition of property to be disclaimed. The 1978 Disclaimer Act includes virtually the same definition of property that can be disclaimed as the other two Acts do.

2. 1999 Uniform Act

The 1999 Disclaimer Act, on the other hand, broadened the scope of the 1978 Acts. To begin with, under Section 3, the 1999 Disclaimer Act "applies to disclaimers of any interest in or power over property whenever created." Section 4 states that principles of law and equity supplement the 1999 Disclaimer Act unless "displaced by a provision" of the Act. Further, Section 4(b) points out that the Act does not limit "any right of a person to waive, release, disclaim, or renounce an interest in or power over property under a law other than" the Act.

11. N.Y. CLS EPTL § 2-1.11(c) (McKinney's 2011).
12. *Id.*

Section 5 of the 1999 Disclaimer Act, dealing in part with the types of property that can be disclaimed, is perhaps the most important section of the Act. First, Section 5(a) states that a person may "disclaim, in whole or in part, any interest in or power over property, including a power of appointment, even if its creator imposed a spendthrift provision on transfer or a restriction or limitation on the right to disclaim." Following the principle behind all disclaimers that no one can be forced to accept property, this subsection makes ineffective "any attempt to limit the right to disclaim which the creator of an interest or non-fiduciary power seeks to impose on a person." It broadens prior law so that any sort of power, even contingent remainder interests in trusts, may be disclaimed.

Subsection (b) addresses the disclaimer powers held by fiduciaries. Unless a fiduciary's right to disclaim is "expressly restricted or limited by another statute . . . or by the instrument creating the fiduciary relationship," a fiduciary may disclaim, in whole or in part, "any interest in or power over property, including a power of appointment, whether acting in a personal or representative capacity." As with individuals, the ability to disclaim exists even if the creator "imposed a spendthrift provision or similar restriction." The Comment points out that the fiduciary also has broad disclaimer powers. A trustee "who is also one of several beneficiaries of a trust may have the power to invade trust principal for the beneficiaries." The trustee may disclaim this power as trustee or may disclaim as a holder of a power of appointment under another section.

Subsection (d) specifically allows a partial disclaimer of property or a power. A partial disclaimer "may be expressed as a fraction, percentage, monetary amount, term of years, limitation of a power, or any other interest or estate in property." Further, a disclaimant may disclaim "specific acreage or an undivided fraction or carve out a life estate or remainder from a larger interest in real or personal property." However, the Comment also points out that a disclaimer that "carves out" a remainder or life estate is not a "qualified disclaimer" for purposes of Section 2518.

3. California Law

California Probate Code Section 267 defines "interest" in the context of what can be disclaimed. An "interest" includes "the whole of any property, real or personal, legal or equitable, or any fractional part, share, or particular portion or specific assets thereof, or any estate in any such property, or any power to appoint, consume, apply, or expend property, or any other right, power, privilege, or immunity relating to property." The statute goes on to provide a fairly comprehensive list of items that specifically can be disclaimed.

4. Texas Law

Texas law provides a definition of "property" that can be disclaimed that is perhaps equally broad as California's, though without providing a list. It includes "all legal and equitable interests, powers, and property, whether present or future, whether vested or contingent, and whether beneficial or burdensome, in whole or in part."[13] Partial disclaimers are allowed; "provided, however, that a partial disclaimer shall be effective only with respect to property expressly described or referred to by category in such disclaimer." Additionally, "a partial disclaimer of property which is subject to a burdensome interest created by the decedent's will shall not be effective unless such property constitutes a gift which is separate and distinct from undisclaimed gifts."[14] In *Barrows v. Ezer*,[15] a testator bequeathed real property to devisee, but the devisee disclaimed the bequest *before* the testator's death. The court held that the Texas disclaimer statute was broad enough to make this "earlier in time" disclaimer valid.

5. New York Law

The general rule of a renunciation in New York is that a beneficiary of a disposition may renounce all or part of his interest. However, a surviving tenant or tenant by the entirety may not renounce any portion of the joint property allocable to amounts contributed by that tenant. Under New York law, a "disposition" that can be disclaimed also is defined broadly; it includes many specific items

13. Tex. Prob. Code § 37A (Vernon's 2011).
14. Tex. Prob. Code § 37A(l) (Vernon's 2011).
15. 668 S.W.2d 854 (Tex. App. Houston 14th Dist. 1984).

(such as jointly owned property, dispositions created by powers of appointment and employee benefits plans) as well as any other transfer created "by any testamentary or non testamentary instrument, or by operation of law, at any of the forgoing created or increased by reason of a renunciation made by another person."[16]

6. Distinctions between State Laws

The question of whether a trustee can disclaim a power in trust obviously is an important one. The 1999 Disclaimer Act specifically addressed the issue by broadening the definition contained in the 1978 Acts. California's broad definition allows for the disclaimer of powers held by a fiduciary. Although its definition is less broad than that of California, Texas also appears to allow disclaimers of powers. New York, on the other hand, does not appear to allow a renunciation of fiduciary powers.

D. How to Disclaim?

1. 1978 Uniform Acts

There are three categories of requirements to have an effective disclaimer under the Wills Act. First, a disclaimer must be in writing; and it must include the following: a description of the property, a declaration of the extent of the disclaimer, and the disclaimant's signature. The Wills Act also seems to require a statement that the disclaimer is a "qualified" disclaimer for federal gift tax purposes if that is the disclaimant's intent. Second, the written disclaimer must be delivered in person or mailed by "registered or certified mail" either to a fiduciary of the decedent or the holder of the property. It can, but need not be, recorded. Third, delivery must occur either nine months after the decedent's death (or the death of the donee of a power) or nine months after the "event that determines that the taker of the property or interest has become finally ascertained and his interest indefeasibly vested" in the case of future interests.

16. N.Y. CLS EPTL § 2-1.11(a)(1) (McKinney's 2011).

There also is a caveat that a post–December 31, 1976 disclaimer must be delivered "not later than nine months of the later of the date that the transfer is made or the day on which the person disclaiming attains age twenty-one." This latter provision was intended as a "savings" clause for purposes of Section 2518. Otherwise, the Wills Act permits a disclaimer within nine months after the death of the transferor to be effective for property law purposes, even though it may not be effective for federal tax purposes.

The Nontestamentary Act continues the same writing, timing, and delivery requirement as under the Wills Act, and it has a similar savings clause. The three requirements (writing, delivery, and timing), therefore, apply equally to disclaimers under the Nontestamentary Act as those under the Wills Act, making only the necessary adjustments to account for the fact that the one deals with inter vivos transfers while the other deals with testamentary transfers.

The 1978 Disclaimer Act includes essentially the same requirements for writing, timing, and delivery for disclaimers as those included in the Wills Act and the Nontestamentary Act.

2. 1999 Uniform Act

Subsection 5(c) of the 1999 Disclaimer Act contains five requirements: (1) the writing or other record requirement; (2) the declaration of disclaimer requirement; (3) the description of interest or power requirement; (4) the signature requirement (which allows for electronic signatures); and (5) the delivery requirement. These requirements are similar, but not identical, to those under the 1978 Acts. The Comments contain extensive examples of these requirements. The most important change, as already noted, is that the "timeliness" requirement is significantly changed; it no longer is linked to the nine-month date as set forth in Section 2518. Rather, it is timely if it has not been barred for some other reason (for example, if the disclaimant already has accepted benefits from the property to be disclaimed).

3. California Law

Under California Probate Code Section 278, disclaimer "shall be in writing, shall be signed by the disclaimant, and shall: (a) Identify the creator of the interest; (b) Describe the interest to be disclaimed; (c) State the disclaimer and the extent of the disclaimer." Further, under California Probate Code Section 280, a disclaimer shall be filed with (1) the superior court in the county in which the estate of the decedent is administered (or if there is no administration, the court in any county in which administration would be proper); (2) the trustee, personal representative, other fiduciary, or person responsible for distributing the interest to the beneficiary; (3) any other person having custody or possession of or legal title to the interest; or (4) the creator of the interest.

The fact that a disclaimer is recorded but not filed does not affect the validity of any transaction with respect to the real property or the obligation secured thereby, and the general recording laws govern the transaction.[17]

Like the 1999 Disclaimer Act, California law has no nine-month delivery requirement. Rather, a disclaimer must be filed "within a reasonable time after the person able to disclaim acquires knowledge of the interest." However, there is a conclusive presumption of timely filing if it is filed within nine months of the occurrence of several relevant events.[18]

4. Texas Law

Unlike the 1999 Disclaimer Act, the statutory disclaimer process in Texas is exclusive: "[F]ailure to comply with the provisions hereof shall render such disclaimer ineffective except as an assignment of such property to those who would have received same had the person attempting the disclaimer died prior to the decedent."[19] Texas also has a more formal writing requirement: A disclaimer must be "evidenced by a written memorandum, acknowledged before a notary public or other person authorized to take acknowledgements of conveyances of real estate."[20] Texas also has, unlike California and the 1999 Disclaimer Act, a fairly rigid nine-month filing requirement; a disclaimer of a present interest "shall be filed

17. Cal. Prob. Code § 280(b) (West 2011).
18. *Id.* at § 279.
19. *Id.*
20. Tex. Prob. Code § 37A(h) (Vernon's 2011).

not later than nine months after the death of the decedent," and a "written memorandum of disclaimer disclaiming a future interest may be filed not later than nine months after the event determining that the taker of the property or interest is finally ascertained and his interest is indefeasibly vested."[21] There are certain limited exceptions if the beneficiary is a charitable organization or a governmental agency.

The filing requirement in Texas also is more formal; a written memorandum of disclaimer must be filed "in the probate court in which the decedent's will has been probated or in which proceedings have been commenced for the administration of the decedent's estate or which has before it an application for either of the same." If no administration proceeding has been commenced, the disclaimer

> shall be filed with the county clerk of the county of the decedent's residence, or, if the decedent is not a resident of this state but real property or an interest therein located in this state is disclaimed, a written memorandum of disclaimer shall be filed with the clerk of the county in which such real property or interest therein is located, and recorded by such county clerk in the deed records of that county.[22]

Further, a copy of the disclaimer memorandum shall be delivered in person, or mailed by registered or certified mail, to the legal representative of the transferor of the interest or the holder of legal title to the disclaimed property. Delivery of this copy is subject to the same nine-month period as recordation of it.[23] Once filed and served, it is irrevocable.[24]

5. New York Law

New York, like Texas, has a more formal delivery and filing requirement. A renunciation must be in writing, must be signed and

21. *Id.*
22. Tex. Prob. Code § 37A(h-1) (Vernon's 2011).
23. Tex. Prob. Code § 37A(i) (Vernon's 2011).
24. Tex. Prob. Code § 37A(k) (Vernon's 2011).

acknowledged by the person renouncing, and must be filed in the office "of the clerk of the court having jurisdiction over the will or trust agreement"; or, if there is no such court, then it must be filed in a surrogate's court provided by law as the place of probate or administration of a decedent's estate. This renunciation must be filed within nine months after the effective date of the disposition (typically the date of death of the transferor, or the date of the trust agreement creating the disclaimed interest).[25]

The New York statute also includes specific, unique requirements. First, the renunciation must include an affidavit of the renouncing party that he has not received and is not to receive any consideration for the renunciation (unless authorized by the court). Second, notice of the renunciation must be served personally or as directed by the court, "or upon any other person having custody or possession of or legal title to the property, an interest in which is being renounced"; the time to file and serve the renunciation may be extended on a petition showing reasonable cause and on notice to such persons "and in such manner as the court may direct." Third, the time limit for filing and serving the renunciation is "exclusive," and shall not be suspended or otherwise affected by any other provision of law."[26]

Once filed, a renunciation made under the statute is irrevocable.[27] The statute, however, does not "abridge the right of any beneficiary or other person to assign, convey, release or renounce any property or interest therein arising under any other section of this chapter or other statute or under common law."[28]

6. Distinctions between State Laws

The formal requirements of a disclaimer demonstrate the most significant differences between the various state laws, and provide the greatest traps for the unwary practicing in multiple jurisdictions. California, and states that have adopted the 1999 Disclaimer Act, have much less formal requirements than states like Texas

25. N.Y. CLS EPTL § 2-1.11(c)(2) (McKinney's 2011).
26. *Id.*
27. N.Y. CLS EPTL § 2-1.11(h) (McKinney's 2011).
28. N.Y. CLS EPTL § 2-1.11(i) (McKinney's 2011).

and New York, for instance. The latter have fairly strict nine-month delivery requirements, and each requires that the disclaimer be filed with the appropriate court. Failure to do so will result in an ineffective disclaimer.

E. What Is the Disclaimer's Effect?

The next issue, once the disclaimer has been made, is the effect of that disclaimer. Specifically, does the doctrine of "relation back" apply?

1. 1978 Uniform Acts

Section 3 of the Wills Act provides that, if the transferor of the property being disclaimed (including a decedent or donee of a power) has provided for an alternate disposition in the event of disclaimer, that disposition controls. If there is no such alternate disposition, then the property passes "as if the disclaimant had predeceased the decedent or, if the disclaimant is designated to take under a power of appointment . . . , as if the disclaimant had predeceased the donee of the power," or "as if the disclaimant had died before the event determining that the taker of the property or interest had become finally ascertained and his interest indefeasibly vested."

Case law provides that the disclaimer of rights as a life insurance policy beneficiary does not bar the disclaimant from being the beneficiary of the insured's intestate estate, and a separate disclaimer must be made of interests passing by testate or intestate succession.[29] It also provides that, because the disclaimer scheme in the Wills Act is comprehensive, "equitable" principles cannot apply; a unilateral mistake as to the legal effect of a disclaimer cannot be corrected by either revocation or reformation.[30]

The Comments to Section 3 clarify that property following a disclaimer passes in a manner similar to that of a lapsed gift and

29. *See, e.g.*, Barker v. Jackson Nat. Life Ins. Co., 888 F. Supp. 1131 (N.D. Fla. 1995).

30. *See, e.g.*, Fleenor v. Williamson, 171 Or. App. 599, 17 P.3d 520 (2000).

that "a renunciation of a devise or legacy relates to the date of death of the decedent or donee and prevents the succession from becoming operative in favor of the disclaimant." This relation-back principle applies *for all purposes*, regardless of motive; and it is "immaterial that the affect [of the disclaimer] is to avoid the imposition of a higher death tax than would be the case if the interest had been accepted," or if the effect is to frustrate a creditor. Indeed, a creditor may not even be entitled to notice of the disclaimer.[31]

Those Comments also provide that, if a life estate or other future interest is disclaimed, the remainder interests are accelerated, and "any future interest . . . takes effect as if the disclaimant had predeceased the event which determines that the taker has become finally ascertained and his interest indefeasibly vested." This, of course, is the result only if the dispositive instrument does not provide otherwise. Finally, Section 4(c) makes clear that the disclaimer or the written waiver of the right to disclaim is binding not only on the disclaimant but also on all persons claiming through or under him. Section 3 of the Nontestamentary Act parallels the provision of the corresponding section in the Wills Act, and Sections 4(a) and (b) of the 1978 Disclaimer Act include the relation-back principle codified in the other two Acts. Section 4(c) mirrors the other two Acts by making clear that a disclaimer is binding "upon the disclaimant or person waiving and all persons claiming through or under him."

2. 1999 Uniform Act

The 1999 Disclaimer Act clarifies many of the principles in the 1978 Acts. According to the Comment, Subsection 5(f) "restates the long standing rule that a disclaimer is a true refusal to accept and not an act by which the disclaimant transfers, assigns, or releases the disclaimed interest." As a result, this subsection "states the effect and meaning of the traditional 'relation back' doctrine of prior Acts."

Section 6 of the 1999 Disclaimer Act sets forth rules that apply to disclaimers of interests in property. Except for disclaimers of jointly owned property and interests in trust, a disclaimer "takes

31. *In re* Est. of Hansen, 109 Ill. App. 2d 283, 248 N.E.2d 709 (1969).

effect as of the time the instrument creating the interest becomes irrevocable, or, if the interest arose under the law of intestate succession, as of the time of the intestate's death." The disclaimed interest "passes according to any provision in the instrument creating the interest providing for the disposition of the interest, should it be disclaimed, or of disclaimed interests in general." If there is no such provision, then if the disclaimant is an individual, "the disclaimed interest passes as if the disclaimant had died immediately before the time of distribution." If the disclaimant is not an individual, then the disclaimed interest passes as if the disclaimant did not exist.

"Time of distribution" means the time when "a disclaimed interest would have taken effect in possession or enjoyment." The Comment to Section 6 states that the "time of distribution of present interests created by will and all interests arising under the law of intestate succession is the death of the decedent." However, the "time of distribution of present interests created by non-testamentary instruments generally depends on when the instrument becomes irrevocable. Because the recipient of a present interest is entitled to the property as soon as the gift is made, the time of distribution occurs when the creator of the interest can no longer take it back." That Comment also states that the 1999 Disclaimer Act "continues the effect of the relation back doctrine not by using the specific words, but by directly stating what the relation back doctrine has been interpreted to mean." By combining Sections 2(3), 5(f), and 6(b)(1), a disclaimer is a refusal to accept, which is not a transfer or release that is effective as of the time the interest was created. This is exactly the effect of relation back without adopting the term per se.

Section 6(b)(4) states that, following the disclaimer of a preceding interest, "a future interest held by a person other than the disclaimant takes effect as if the disclaimant had died or ceased to exist immediately before the time of distribution, but a future interest held by the disclaimant is not accelerated in possession or enjoyment." The issues surrounding acceleration are discussed in greater detail below.

The Comments also clarify the effect of an attempted disclaimer that is barred by this section over a power or property interest. Although the disclaimer is ineffective, it operates as a transfer of the disclaimed property, and the person attempting the disclaimer will bear any transfer tax consequences. Section 14 of the 1999 Disclaimer Act and the Comment thereunder provide that a disclaimer that is qualified for estate and gift tax purposes is valid even if it does not otherwise meet more specific requirements under the 1999 Disclaimer Act.

3. California Law

California also adopts the relation-back concept: A disclaimer "relates back for all purposes to the date of the death of the creator of the disclaimed interest or the determinative event, as the case may be."[32] Further, an heir cannot disclaim property for the purpose of increasing the share of his or her lineal descendants at the expense of the lines of other descendants.[33] California law also contains a fairly unique provision: A disclaimer "is not a fraudulent transfer by the beneficiary."[34] A more complete discussion of the state law of fraudulent conveyance with respect to disclaimers is set forth below. Finally, if a disclaimer is effective under Section 2518, then it is valid under California law.

4. Texas Law

In Texas, unless a decedent's will provides otherwise, property subject to a disclaimer "shall pass as if the person disclaiming or on whose behalf a disclaimer is made had predeceased the decedent and the future interest that would otherwise take effect in possession or enjoyment after the termination of the estate or interest that is disclaimed takes effect as if the disclaiming beneficiary had predeceased the decedent."[35] A Texas disclaimer "shall relate back for all purposes to the death of the decedent," and the disclaimed property "is not subject to the claims of any creditor of the disclaimant."[36]

---

32. Cal. Prob. Code § 282 (West 2011).
33. Cal. Prob. Code § 282(b) (West 2011).
34. Cal. Prob. Code § 283 (West 2011).
35. Tex. Prob. Code § 37A(c) (Vernon's 2011).
36. Tex. Prob. Code § 37A(b) (Vernon's 2011).

5. New York Law

In New York, unless the creator of the disposition provided otherwise, a valid renunciation "has the same effect with respect to the renounced interest as though the renouncing person had predeceased the creator or the decedent." If the renounced interest is a future estate, the effect is as though the renouncing person had died at the time of filing or just before the future estate becoming an estate in possession, whichever is earlier, and has the effect of accelerating the possession and enjoyment of subsequent interests. However, the renunciation of the future estate has no effect upon the vesting of a future estate that, by the terms of the disposition, is limited upon a proceeding estate other than the renounced interest.[37] If pursuant to renunciation a per stirpes disposition of the renounced interest occurs, than the renouncing person is treated as having died on the same day as, but immediately after, the creator or decedent. In this case, if the renounced interest is a future estate, the renounced person is treated as having died on the same day as, but immediately after, the interest becoming an estate in possession or on the same day as, but immediately after, the time of filing, whichever is earlier. The renunciation is retroactive to the creation of the disposition.[38]

A person who has a present and a future interest in property and renounces either in whole or in part the present interest is deemed to have renounced the future interest to the same extent.[39] A beneficiary may accept one disposition and renounce another or may renounce a disposition in whole or in part (including with reference to specific amounts, parts, fractional interests, or assets thereof). Unless the renouncing party has provided otherwise, the effect of a fractional renunciation is to renounce such fraction of all property to which the renouncing party is entitled under the disposition.[40]

Finally, the renunciation by a surviving spouse of a disposition created by the predeceased spouse is not deemed to be a

37. N.Y. CLS EPTL § 2-1.11(e) (McKinney's 2011).
38. *Id.*
39. *Id.*
40. N.Y. CLS EPTL § 2-1.11(f) (McKinney's 2011).

renunciation by the surviving spouse of "all or any part of any other disposition to or in favor of such spouse, regardless of whether the property which would have passed under said renounced disposition is by reason of said renunciation disposed of to or in favor of such spouse."[41]

6. Distinctions between State Laws

The laws of all states are similar in their application of the relation-back principle (even though those states that have adopted the 1999 Disclaimer Act do not state it explicitly). Perhaps the biggest difference is that some states, like California and Texas, provide explicitly that a disclaimer is either not a fraudulent conveyance or is not subject to creditor claims. Although in theory the relation-back principle should render such a statement moot, it may be that this type of statutory distinction will have greater meaning in the future.

F. What Bars a Disclaimer?

State law provides circumstances under which a disclaimer is barred. Some of them are similar to those under federal law: Many states bar an attempted disclaimer that occurs more than nine months after the transfer of the property sought to be disclaimed, and all states bar a disclaimer of property, the benefits of which already have been accepted by the would-be disclaimant. However, the state statutes can vary significantly.

1. 1978 Uniform Acts

Under Section 4(a) of the Wills Act, the ability to disclaim property can be barred by (1) an assignment, conveyance, encumbrance, pledge, or transfer of the property (or a contract therefor); (2) a written waiver of the right to disclaim; (3) acceptance of the property or a benefit thereunder; or (4) a judicial sale of the property made before the disclaimer is effected. However, the right to

---

41. *Id.*

disclaim exists notwithstanding any restriction "in the nature of a spendthrift provision or similar restriction." This is consistent with the concept of relation back because, if the disclaimant is deemed never to have owned the property, then no such limitation should apply.

Further, a disclaimer under the Wills Act must be made within a set period of time or it is barred. Section 2 of the Wills Act addresses both the time in which a disclaimer must be made and the required method of delivery. This time frame changes, depending on whether the property being disclaimed is a present or future interest. An instrument disclaiming a present interest "shall be delivered not later than nine months after the death of the decedent or the donee of the power." An instrument disclaiming a future interest "shall be delivered not later than nine months after the event that determines that the taker of the property or interest has become finally ascertained and his interest is indefeasibly vested." However, these two requirements are subject to the overall caveat that the disclaimer of a transfer creating an interest in the disclaimant that was made after December 31, 1976, and subject to federal transfer taxes must specifically state that it is intended to be a qualified disclaimer under Section 2518 and must be delivered "not later than nine months of the later of the date that the transfer is made or the day on which the person disclaiming attains age twenty-one." This latter provision was intended as a "savings" clause. The Section 2518 requirements are incorporated into a disclaimer under the Wills Act only if the transferor dies after 1976 and the disclaimant intends his disclaimer to be effective for federal tax purposes. Otherwise, the Wills Act permits a disclaimer within nine months after the death of the transferor to be effective for property law purposes, even though it may not be effective for federal tax purposes.

With respect to the Nontestamentary Act, Section 2 includes similar timing and delivery requirements as Section 2 of the Wills Act, except that the delivery must occur nine months after the "effective date of the nontestamentary instrument" rather than nine months after the donor's death. Further, if the person entitled to claim has no actual knowledge of the existence of the interest, "the instrument of disclaimer shall be delivered not later than nine months after he has actual knowledge of the existence of the interest." Note that this "actual knowledge" time frame does not apply if the disclaimer is made after December 31, 1976, and is subject to federal transfer taxes. In that case, the disclaimer must state that it is intended to be a qualified disclaimer and must be delivered "not later than nine months after the later of the date the transfer is made or the day on which the person disclaiming attains age twenty-one." Finally, Section 4 of the Nontestamentary Act, listing the bars to disclaimer, is virtually identical to that in the Wills Act.

The bars to disclaimer in the 1978 Disclaimer Act follows those of the other two 1978 Acts. Section 2(a) includes essentially the same requirements for timing of a disclaimer and delivery for disclaimers of property transferred under a testamentary instrument as those included in the Wills Act. Section 2(b) includes identical timing and delivery requirements for non-testamentary transfers as under the Nontestamentary Act. In both cases, the disclaimer must take place nine months after the date of death of the deceased owner of property or the transfer of the property interest, as the case may be for present interests. Also, this period is extended until nine months after the date of actual knowledge of the existence of the interest in the case of the non-testamentary transfers, but not testamentary transfers. Section 2(c) overrides the first two provisions for transfers made after December 31, 1976, and subject to federal transfer taxes. In this case, a disclaimer that is intended as a "qualified" disclaimer "must specifically so state and must be delivered not later than nine months after the later of the date the transfer is made or the day on which the person disclaiming attains age twenty-one." Section 5 of the 1978 Disclaimer Act includes the same "no acceptance" rule as in the other two Acts: A person cannot disclaim property if she has assigned, conveyed, or transferred the property, has waived in writing the right to disclaim, has accepted the property or an interest or benefit thereunder, or there has been a judicial sale of the property.

2. 1999 Uniform Act

The bars to disclaimer under the 1999 Disclaimer Act are different from those in the 1978 Acts. The most important difference is the elimination of the nine-month time limit.

Section 13 provides the conditions under which a disclaimer is barred or limited. First, a disclaimer is barred by a written waiver of the right to disclaim. Second, a disclaimer of an interest in property is barred if any of the following events occur before the disclaimer becomes effective:

- The disclaimant accepts the interest sought to be disclaimed;
- The disclaimant voluntarily assigns, conveys, encumbers, pledges, or transfers the interest sought to be disclaimed or contracts to do so; or
- There is a judicial sale of the interest sought to be disclaimed.
- A disclaimer, either in whole or in part, of the future exercise of a fiduciary power is not barred by its previous exercise.
- A disclaimer, in whole or in part, of the future exercise of a power *not* held in a fiduciary capacity also is not barred by its previous exercise, unless the power is exercisable in favor of the disclaimant.
- A disclaimer is barred or limited if it is so provided by law other than under the 1999 Disclaimer Act.

Section 13(f) states that a disclaimer of a power "over property which is barred by this Section is ineffective." The transfer is negated; it takes effect "as a transfer of the interest to be disclaimed to the persons who would have not taken the interest . . . had the disclaimer not been barred."

Section 13 represents one of the substantial changes from the 1978 Acts. As the Comments point out, this section specifically rejects a time requirement for making a disclaimer. Recognizing that disclaimers are used for purposes other than tax planning, a disclaimer can be made effectively under the 1999 Disclaimer Act so long as the disclaimant is not barred from disclaiming the property or interest or has not waived the right to disclaim. This now puts the onus on the disclaimant and his or her advisors to ensure that, if they seek to make a disclaimer that qualifies under Section 2518, they must ensure that they have met the qualifications without the safety net of a state statute.

An important bar to a disclaimer under the 1999 Disclaimer Act is the acceptance of the property sought to be disclaimed. The 1999 Disclaimer Act adds the word "voluntary" to transfers, assigns, encumbrances, and so forth. This reflects "the numerous cases holding that only actions by the disclaimant taken after the right to disclaim has arisen will act as a bar." Therefore, an existing lien does not prevent a disclaimer.[42] However, the disclaimant's actions before the right to disclaim arises may create estoppel. Further, with regard to joint property the death of the joint holder creates the right to disclaim, not the creation of the joint interest. Therefore, any benefit received during the deceased joint tenant's life is ignored. Note that this is a state law issue only. The prohibition of disclaimer following judicial sale, according to the Comments, "ensures the title gained from a judicial sale by a personal representative will not be clouded by a possible disclaimer." This begs the question, however, of why the proceeds could not be disclaimed once the sale had begun. Under Section 13(e), a disclaimer is barred by statutes other than this one or by case law in the various states.

The Comments also clarify the effect of an attempted disclaimer over a power or property interest that is barred by this section. In this case, although the disclaimer is ineffective, it operates as a transfer of the disclaimed property interest to the persons who would have taken had the disclaimer not been barred. The person attempting the disclaimer will bear any transfer tax consequences.

3. California Law

California law shares some of these features with the 1999 Disclaimer Act. There is no nine-month limitation on disclaimers. However, the right to disclaim can end under California law if a written waiver of that right is filed,[43] or if the interest sought to be

42. *See* Hale v. Bardouh, 975 S.W.2d 419 (Tex. Ct. App. 1998).
43. Cal. Prob. Code § 284 (West 2011).

disclaimed has been accepted.[44] On the other hand, the right to disclaim is not affected by a spendthrift provision.[45]

4. Texas Law

Unlike California and the 1999 Disclaimer Act, a Texas disclaimer of a present interest "shall be filed not later than nine months after the death of the decedent," and a "written memorandum of disclaimer disclaiming a future interest may be filed not later than nine months after the event determining that the taker of the property or interest is finally ascertained and his interest is indefeasibly vested."[46] Therefore, failing to do so is a bar to disclaimer. There is an exception to this rule if the beneficiary is a charitable organization or a governmental agency; in this case, a written memorandum of disclaimer "shall be filed not later than nine months after the beneficiary receives the notice required by" Section 128A of the Texas Probate Code. The statutory disclaimer process in Texas is exclusive: "[F]ailure to comply with the provisions hereof shall render such disclaimer ineffective except as an assignment of such property to those who would have received same had the person attempting the disclaimer died prior to the decedent."[47]

As with virtually every other jurisdiction, acceptance under Texas law is a bar to disclaimer. A disclaimer is not effective "after the acceptance of the property by the beneficiary." Acceptance occurs "only if the person making such disclaimer has previously taken possession or exercised dominion and control of such property in the capacity of beneficiary."[48]

5. New York Law

In New York, a renunciation must be filed within nine months after the effective date of the disposition.[49] As in all other jurisdictions, a person cannot renounce any property that he has accepted, except

44. Cal. Prob. Code § 285 (West 2011).
45. Cal. Prob. Code § 286 (West 2011).
46. Tex. Prob. Code § 37A(h) (Vernon's 2011).
47. Tex. Prob. Code § 37A(d) (Vernon's 2011).
48. Tex. Prob. Code § 37A(n) (Vernon's 2011).
49. N.Y. CLS EPTL § 2.1.11(c)(2) (McKinney's 2011).

that an acceptance does not preclude that person "from renouncing all or part of any property to which he becomes entitled when another person renounces after such acceptance." Acceptance occurs under the statute if the renouncing party "voluntarily transfers or encumbers, or contracts to transfer or encumber all or part of such interest, or accepts delivery or payment of, or exercises control as beneficial owner over all or part thereof, or executes a written waiver of the right to renounce, or otherwise indicates acceptance of all or part of such interest."[50] A written waiver of the right to renounce is binding upon the person executing the waiver and all parties claiming by, through, or under him.[51]

---

50. N.Y. CLS EPTL § 2-1.11(g) (McKinney's 2011).
51. *Id.*

3 STATE DISCLAIMER LAWS—PARTICULAR INTERESTS

Disclaimers of outright gifts, either during life or at death, are set forth in a fairly straightforward fashion in most statutes. More difficult is the question of disclaimers of jointly held assets or of fiduciary powers or powers of appointment. This chapter addresses these particular "problem" disclaimers.

A. Jointly Held Interests

The Wills Act does not address disclaimers of jointly held interests in any detail; Section 1 states that a person may disclaim "the right of succession to any property or interest therein," and such disclaimer "may be of a fractional share or any limited interest or estate." The Comments to that section simply state that the "succession" to any property includes "the right to renounce any survivorship interest in a community property state." The situation of joint tenancy is discussed more clearly in the Nontestamentary Act; however, it leaves open the question of whether the surviving joint tenant has any right to renounce "his interest in jointly-owned property and if so, to what extent."[1] As the Comments to Section 1 of the Nontestamentary Act point out, the Act's position "is to confer the right of disclaimer upon the surviving joint tenant and leave to the particular circumstances whether he may disclaim all of the interest or only the accretive part and the effect of knowledge of the existence of the tenancy, acceptance of benefits, and the like."

The 1978 Act is not especially clear on the right of a surviving joint tenant to disclaim that portion of jointly held property to which the survivor succeeds by operation of law on the death of the other joint tenant (the "accretive share"); Section 1 of that Act states that a person "to whom any property or interest therein devolves, by whatever means, may disclaim it in whole or in part." The Comments to that section state that it "mirrors the provisions of the separate disclaimer Acts and is designed for application in states where the codification system lends itself to a single Act affecting successions and transfers whether derived from testamentary or nontestamentary sources." Further, the Comments made with respect to the other two 1978 Acts "are applicable to" the 1978 Disclaimer Act. Therefore, since the Comments to the Nontestamentary Act provide for a disclaimer by a surviving joint tenant, the 1978 Disclaimer Act should apply with equal force (and equal vagueness on the subject of whether the disclaimant can disclaim his or her own share of the property). Nevertheless, several states have adopted variations from the official text which state specifically that the surviving joint tenant may disclaim joint property.[2]

After the 1978 Uniform Acts were drafted, the law regarding disclaimers of joint property interests was clarified significantly. First, three different circuit courts held that the surviving joint tenant can disclaim the accretive share, so long as the joint ten-

1. Uniform Disclaimer of Transfers Under Nontestamentary Instruments Act, Cmt. Section 1 (1978).

2. *See, e.g.*, Ala. Code §§ 43-8-290 to 43-8-298 (West 2004); 12 Del. C. §§ 6012608 (West 2004).

ancy was severable during the joint tenants' lives.[3] Second, in 1997 the Internal Revenue Service (IRS) issued final regulations with respect to disclaimers of jointly held property.[4]

To account for these changes, Section 7 of the 1999 Disclaimer Act addresses disclaimers of rights of survivorship in jointly held property. Upon the death of a holder of jointly held property, the surviving holder may disclaim in whole or in part the greater of (1) a fractional share of the property determined by dividing the number one by the number of joint holders alive immediately before the death of the holder to whose death the disclaimer relates; or (2) all of the property except that part of the value of the entire interest attributable to the contribution furnished by the disclaimant. Under subsection (b), such a disclaimer takes effect as of the death of the holder of jointly held property to whose death the disclaimer relates. Finally, subsection (c) provides that an interest in jointly held property "disclaimed by a surviving holder of the property passes as if the disclaimant predeceased the holder to whose death the disclaimer relates."

The Comment to Section 7 notes that since the "previous Uniform Acts were drafted, the law regarding tax qualified disclaimers of joint property interests has been clarified." These developments in tax law are reflected in subsection (a). That subsection allows a surviving holder of jointly held property to "disclaim the greater of the accretive share, the part of the jointly-held property which augments the survivor's interest in the property, and all of the property that is not attributable to the disclaimant's contribution to the jointly-held property."

For example, if A contributes 60 percent and B contributes 40 percent to a joint bank account, and they allow the interest on the funds to accumulate, on A's death B can disclaim 40 percent of the account; on B's death A can disclaim 60 percent of the account.

Because the disclaimer is effective as of the death of the joint holder, the Comments point out that the disclaimant "has no

3. *See* Kennedy v. Commissioner, 804 F.2d 1332 (7th Cir. 1986); McDonald v. Commissioner, 853 F.2d 1494 (9th Cir. 1988); Dancy v. Commissioner, 872 F.2d 84 (4th Cir. 1989).

4. Treas. Reg. § 25.2518-2(c)(4)(i).

interest in and has not transferred the disclaimed interest." Further, because the disclaimed interest passes as if the disclaimant had predeceased the holder, if there are two joint holders, the Comment points out that "a disclaimer by the survivor results in the disclaimed property passing as part of the deceased joint holder's estate because under this subsection, the deceased joint holder is the survivor as to the portion disclaimed." So if a married couple owns the family home in joint tenancy, a disclaimer by the survivor under subsection (a)(1) results in one-half of the home passing through the decedent's estate. The surviving spouse and whoever receives the interest through the decedent's estate are tenants in common in the house.

As a further example, assume A, B, and C are joint tenants with right of survivorship in Blackacre. A dies. B then disclaims one-third of the property under subsection (a)(1) divided by 3, the number of joint holders immediately before A's death. B is deemed to have predeceased A, which would leave A and C as the surviving joint owners of the one-third disclaimed. Since A is now dead, C is the sole owner of the one-third that B disclaimed; and C and the joint tenancy as an entity are tenants in common in Blackacre. If B predeceases C, then C will be the sole owner of Blackacre in fee simple. If C predeceases B, then B will own two-thirds of Blackacre outright, and one-third of Blackacre will pass through C's estate.

As already noted, California Probate Code Section 267(b)(11) states that the interest that can be disclaimed includes an interest created by "surviving the death of another joint tenant." Because the interest defined under this statute is only one created by survivorship, that would imply that it includes only the accretive share passing to the surviving joint tenant as a result of the death of the predeceased joint tenant, and not the share attributable to contributions from the surviving joint tenant.

Texas law provides that a "beneficiary" who is entitled to disclaim includes a person who had the right to receive property, in the absence of the disclaimer, as a result of the death of another person by "a joint tenancy with a right of survivorship." As with California, Texas law appears to limit the disclaimer only to the accretive share acquired by the surviving joint tenant as a result of the death of the predeceased joint tenant.[5]

Finally, under New York law, a "disposition" includes a transfer created by a joint tenancy or tenancy by the entirety."[6] However, unlike the other statutes cited, New York law is very specific about what a joint tenant can and cannot disclaim: "A surviving joint tenant or tenant by the entirety may renounce the interest to which such tenant succeeds, by operation of law upon the death of another joint tenant or tenant by the entirety, to the extent such interest could be the subject of a qualified disclaimer" under Section 2518.[7]

B. Fiduciary Powers

The question of disclaimers by fiduciaries is even more problematic than that of disclaimers of jointly held interests. A trustee may wish, for example, to disclaim the power to distribute property among beneficiaries if such power would cause the property to be includable in the trustee's taxable estate (for example, because the power may constitute a "general power of appointment" under Section 2041). Further, for a trust to qualify as "qualified terminable interest property" under Section 2056(b)(7), a trustee is restricted in the kinds of powers he or she may possess: A trustee must have the power to make property productive of income, for example, and cannot have the power to distribute property to anyone other than the surviving spouse. The most obvious use for such disclaimers is those situations in which the holding of a power in the hands of a particular trustee might result in adverse transfer tax consequences. For example, the trustee of a trust for the benefit of a surviving spouse who also has the power to invade principal for other beneficiaries may want to disclaim that power so that the

5. Tex. Prob. Code § 37A (Vernon's 2011).
6. N.Y. CLS EPTL § 2-1.11(b)(1) (McKinney's 2011).
7. N.Y. CLS EPTL § 2-1.11(c)(1) (McKinney's 2011).

trust can qualify for the estate tax marital deduction under Section 2056.[8]

1. STATE LAW

However, it is not clear that trustees have that authority under certain state statutes. For example, none of the 1978 Acts provide specifically for the disclaimer of a power by a fiduciary. The 1999 Disclaimer Act corrects this omission; Section 11 governs disclaimers by fiduciaries of powers held in their fiduciary capacity. Examples of such disclaimers would include a disclaimer of the right to remove and replace a trustee or of the trustee's power to make distributions of income or principal. Section 11(a) states that a fiduciary who disclaims a power held in a fiduciary capacity that has not been exercised takes effect as of the time the instrument creating the power became irrevocable. Section 11(b) states that if a fiduciary "disclaims a power held in a fiduciary capacity which has been exercised, the disclaimer takes effect immediately after the last exercise of the power."

This section also deals with disclaimers of powers held in the fiduciary capacity where there is more than one fiduciary. Section 11(c) states that a disclaimer under this Section "is effective as to another fiduciary if the disclaimer so provides and the fiduciary disclaiming has the authority to bind the estate, trust, or other person for whom the fiduciary is acting." The Comments to this section note that the effect of actions of multiple fiduciaries is left "to the general rules in effect in each State relating to multiple fiduciaries." If, for example, a majority of trustees can make binding decisions under the law of a given state, a disclaimer by two of the three co-trustees of a power is effective. If there is a dissenting trustee, she may follow whatever procedure that is allowable under state law for "disassociating him or herself from the action of the majority."

Section 11 as described by the Comments also makes clear that disclaimers by a single trustee are effective only as to that

8. *See, e.g.*, Cleaveland v. U.S., 62 A.F.T.R.2d 88-5992, 88-1 USTC ¶ 13766 (C.D. Ill. 1988).

disclaiming trustee, unless the disclaimer states otherwise. This would allow one co-trustee to disclaim a certain power while allowing her co-trustees to retain it. Finally, the Comments state that, as with any action by a fiduciary, "a disclaimer of fiduciary powers must be compatible with the fiduciary's duties."

The 1999 Disclaimer Act also allows a trustee to disclaim trust property. Section 8 provides that if a trustee "disclaims an interest in property that otherwise would have become trust property, the interest does not become trust property." The Comment points out that the "instrument under which the right to receive the property was created may govern the disposition of the property in the event of a disclaimer by providing for a disposition when the trust does not exist." However, if the instrument does not make such a provision, "the doctrine of resulting trust will carry the property back to the donor." Actions under this Section 8 by co-trustees will depend upon state law governing actions of multiple trustees. Finally, this section reminds all fiduciaries that any disclaimer they make must be "compatible with the trustee's fiduciary obligations."

Given California's broad definition of an interest that can be disclaimed, it would seem that a fiduciary can disclaim powers held in a fiduciary capacity; under California Probate Code Section 267, "interest" includes "any power to appoint, consume, apply, or expend property, or any other right, power, privilege, or immunity relating to property." That section goes on to state that "interest" includes, but is not limited to, an interest created under a trust.[9] However, California law also states that a "disclaimer" means any writing that disclaims any interest that otherwise would be taken by a "beneficiary,"[10] which is defined as a person entitled, but for the persons disclaimer, to "take an interest."[11] Because the statute deals only with disclaimers by "beneficiaries," this leaves open the question whether it applies to trustees disclaiming fiduciary powers.

Texas law also provides a very broad definition of what can be disclaimed, but does not address specifically whether a trustee or

9. CAL. PROB. CODE § 267(b)(3) (West 2011).
10. CAL. PROB. CODE § 265 (West 2011).
11. CAL. PROB. CODE § 262 (West 2011).

other fiduciary can disclaim a fiduciary power. As already noted, under Texas law the term *property* includes "all legal and equitable interests, powers and property, whether present or future, whether vested or contingent, and whether beneficial or burdensome." However, the statute also states that the disclaimer statute applies to any person "who may be entitled to receive any property as a beneficiary."[12] This certainly implies that the statute allows disclaimers only by beneficiaries, not trustees.

Similarly, New York law defines dispositions that may be renounced in terms of property rights, not fiduciary powers, and provides that any "beneficiary of a disposition" may renounce all or part of his interest.[13]

2. Interaction with Federal Tax Law

Although the question of whether a fiduciary may disclaim fiduciary powers is subtle, it is clear in most jurisdictions that the holder of a power of appointment can disclaim that power. Tax cases and IRS rulings may be helpful in determining when a fiduciary may and may not disclaim a power, and whether or not that disclaimer will work to achieve the desired goal.

For example, the IRS in TAM 9818005 ruled that attempted disclaimers did not create a qualifying income interest for life within the meaning of Section 2056(b)(7). In this case, one half of the decedent's estate passed to a trust for the benefit of the decedent's surviving spouse that qualified for the marital deduction under Section 2056(b)(5). The residue of the decedent's estate passed to a residuary trust that provided that the trustee was to use as much of the income or principal as the trustee deemed necessary for the support and reasonable comfort of the surviving spouse, and to provide for the support and education of the decedent's children. The surviving spouse also had the power to direct the trustee to distribute trust property among the descendants and spouses as the surviving spouse appointed. The trustee had the power to hold for investment unproductive and unimproved real

---

12. TEX. PROB. CODE § 37A(a) (Vernon's 2011).
13. N.Y. CLS EPTL §2-1.11(c)(1) (McKinney's 2011).

estate and to allocate ordinary dividends and gains from sales of unproductive real estate between income and principal as seemed "fair and just." Finally, all of these trustee powers were intended "to apply to each fiduciary named" in the decedent's will. This plan was effective before 1981, when Congress through the Economic Recovery Tax Act provided the unlimited marital deduction. With the unlimited marital deduction, however, the surviving spouse could receive more than half of the estate and qualify for the marital deduction if the trust terms were appropriately drafted.

The surviving spouse petitioned the probate court for authority to "Renounce and Disclaim Interests in Property." The petition provided that guardians ad litem be provided for the minor children of the decedent and for unborn and unascertained descendants. Following that, all beneficiaries of the residuary trust other than the spouse would disclaim their beneficial interests in the trust. Further, the surviving spouse as trustee disclaimed the certain trustee powers that disqualified the trust from the marital deduction, including the power to hold unproductive property.

The IRS noted that "a trustee cannot accept a trust in part and disclaim in part." Further, "a disclaimer by a trustee does not extinguish a power except with respect to the disclaiming fiduciary." It then cited Rev. Rul. 90-10,[14] under which a surviving spouse purported to disclaim her power as trustee to invade corpus for the benefit of the Grantor's grandchild. The grandchild neither disclaimed his interest in trust nor consented to the trustee's disclaimer. Therefore, under applicable local law, "the trustee's attempt to disclaim this type of power was ineffective without written consent of the beneficiary or an express grant of authority to make such a disclaimer in the governing instrument." Therefore, the Revenue Ruling concluded that the trustee's attempted renunciation power to invade corpus was not qualified under local law and therefore was not a qualified disclaimer. Similarly, in the technical advice memorandum situation, the governing instrument did not authorize the disclaimer of trustee powers; indeed, the will provided that the provisions were intended to apply to each

14. 1990-2 C.B. 209.

fiduciary named in the will. Further, under the state statute in question, the fiduciary is allowed "ACTING ON BEHALF OF ANOTHER PERSON [emphasis in original]," to renounce property or an interest in property which was transferred "TO THAT OTHER PERSON [emphasis in original]." This statute, according to the IRS, did not authorize a trustee to disclaim powers and duties; the trustee was not renouncing an interest in property on behalf of another person, but rather was attempting to renounce her own powers and duties that she "possessed by virtue of being the trustee." As a result, the attempted disclaimer of trustee powers and duties was not valid under local law and, therefore, was not a qualified disclaimer.

Similarly, PLR 8409024, dealing with Ohio law, held that, although Ohio law allows a fiduciary under a testamentary or non-testamentary instrument to disclaim fiduciary rights, privileges, powers, and immunities, a fiduciary may not disclaim the rights of beneficiaries unless the instrument creating the fiduciary relationship authorizes such a disclaimer. In the case at hand, a decedent's will created a trust for the benefit of his surviving spouse. The trust provided that the surviving spouse was to receive the entire income from the trust; however, during any period in which the trustees determined that the surviving spouse was incapable of "attending to her financial affairs because of any mental or physical ailment," the trustees were directed to distribute only as much of the income as was necessary to provide for her support, care, health, and welfare. The surviving spouse had been adjudicated competent. Therefore, a marital deduction was not available because the surviving spouse did not have a qualifying income interest for life. The trustees attempted to disclaim their power to withhold income if they decided she was incapable of handling her affairs.

The IRS ruled that the power to withhold income was not the type of fiduciary power that can be disclaimed under Ohio law. The ability to withhold income, on the other hand, was a "mandatory power," the exercise of which was intended to, and does, directly affect the beneficial interests involved. Further, even if the Ohio law allowing the disclaimer of discretionary powers to apply to this power, the proposed disclaimer would not eliminate or extinguish the disclaimed powers. A fiduciary disclaimer "only has the affect of freeing the disclaiming fiduciary from exercising the power." It must then be exercised by successor fiduciaries. Therefore, not only was the disclaimer ineffective, but even if it had been effective, it still would not have been adequate to change the terms of the trust.

Finally, in a tax court case addressing the marital deduction,[15] the court held that a proposed disclaimer by trustees of certain powers granted to them by the trust instrument was ineffective. The court held that, under Kansas law, powers given to a trustee to transfer title to trust property can be exercised only in the manner and under the express conditions specified in the trust instrument. Further, the trustee cannot accept the trust in part and disclaim in part. The trustees were attempting to disclaim the power to terminate a trust if it contained assets with a value of less than $100,000. The court held that the trustees were attempting to "substitute their view of what the decedent intended for the clearly written language" of the trust agreement. The trustees, the court held, were "attempting to disclaim powers, duties, and discretions that would amount to a renunciation of their trusteeships." This renunciation cannot be effective, particularly where it is done "solely for the purpose of changing the Federal tax results of this case."

The news is not all bad, however. In PLR 8815038, a disclaimer by the decedent's children as beneficiaries (not as trustees) of the trustees power to make loans of trust principal upon any terms to any person were effective, and therefore the trust would qualify for the marital deduction. Similarly, in PLR 200028020, the IRS addressed a situation in which a decedent executed a will and was survived by a spouse, three children, grandchildren, and nieces. Under the terms of the will, the residue of his estate passed to a trust, which was to be divided into a marital trust and a residuary distribution. The marital trust was to be funded with the smallest amount, after taking into account all allowable credits and deductions available to the decedent's estate, to reduce the total tax payable to the greatest extent possible. The remaining trust property

15. Est. of Bennett, 100 T.C. 42 (1993).

was distributable in percentages to children, grandchildren, and nieces. Two of the children (both as beneficiaries and trustees of the trust), the grandchildren, and nieces executed disclaimers of some portion of their rights to receive property under the decedent's will and trust. As a result of these disclaimers, the property passed to a third child. Note that, as in the prior ruling, the disclaimers of the trustee powers were made by the beneficiaries as well as the trustees.

As the preceding discussion shows, it may not be clear from state to state whether a trustee can disclaim either a fiduciary power or an interest in a trust. Unless a client resides in a state that has adopted the 1999 Disclaimer Act or similar statute, it may be helpful to have the trustee disclaim a given power and have the beneficiaries disclaim their rights to receive the benefit of the exercise or non-exercise of the power.

C. Powers of Appointment

Section 1 of the Wills Act grants to a person who is an "appointee under a power of appointment exercised by a testamentary instrument" the power to disclaim that interest. Section 1 of the Nontestamentary Act and Section 1 of the 1978 Disclaimer Act both provide very broad definitions of the property that may be disclaimed, which would include appointees under powers of appointment. Section 9 of the 1999 Disclaimer Act deals with disclaimers of powers of appointment or other powers that are not held in a fiduciary capacity. In the event of such a disclaimer, three rules apply. First, if the holder has not "exercised the power, the disclaimer takes effect as of the time the instrument creating the power becomes irrevocable." Second, if the holder has exercised the power and the disclaimer is of a power "other than a presently exercisable general power of appointment, the disclaimer takes effect immediately after the last exercise of the power." Finally, the instrument creating the power is construed "as if the power expired when the disclaimer became effective." This section again shows the increasing breadth of the 1999 Disclaimer Act over the 1978 Acts. The Comment indicates that "the disclaimer could be of a portion of the power to appoint one's self, while retaining the right to appoint to others."

For example, assume that T creates a testamentary trust to pay the income to A for life, the remainder as A shall appoint by will among her descendants living at A's death and for named charities. If A does not exercise her power, the remainder passes to her descendants living at her death by representation. A disclaims the power. The power can no longer be exercised, and on A's death the remainder will pass to the takers in default.

Section 10 governs disclaimers by beneficiaries who "may or do receive an interest in property through the exercise of a power of appointment." When a power of appointment is created, the creator of the power can not only give the power to the power holder, she also can limit the objects in favor of whom the power can be exercised and name those who take property if the power is not exercised. Section 10(a) states that a "disclaimer of an interest in property by an appointee of a power of appointment takes effect as of the time the instrument by which the holder exercises the power became irrevocable." In other words, if a person is affirmatively designated as a beneficiary under a power of appointment, her disclaimer of any property passing under that appointment becomes effective as of the time the instrument exercising the power becomes irrevocable. So, for example, if the power is exercisable by a will, then a disclaimer of an interest that is to be received as the result of an exercise of the power under the will becomes effective upon the death of the power holder.

Section 10(b) states that a "disclaimer of an interest in property by an object or taker in default of an exercise of a power of appointment takes effect as of the time the instrument creating the power becomes irrevocable."

As another example, assume A creates a trust under her will for the benefit of her daughter, B. Upon B's death, she has the power to appoint the trust property by will among her then-living descendants. In default of this appointment, the property is distributed to B's brother, C. If B exercises her power of appointment in favor of her children and one child disclaims, then the child's disclaimer is effective as of B's death (at which time the will exercising the power becomes irrevocable). On the other hand, if B does not exercise her power of appointment, and C disclaims his interest in the property of the trust for B's benefit, then C's disclaimer becomes effective on the date of A's death (the time that the instrument creating the power, A's will, becomes effective).

Note that in the case of a disclaimer by a taker in default, the effect of the disclaimer is governed by Section 6 because the disclaimer is over an interest in property. On the other hand, for a person who is disclaiming property that is appointed to her by a power holder, the effect of the disclaimer can be governed under Section 6 if the appointment results in the beneficiary receiving property, or under Section 9 if the holder creates another power of appointment in the appointee. The Comments to Section 10 point out that "if all the objects and takers in default disclaim before the power is exercised the power of appointment is destroyed.[16]

Finally, California,[17] Texas,[18] and New York[19] all allow disclaimers of both the power to appoint property and of property to which the disclaimant is entitled as a result of the exercise of a power of appointment.

---

16. *See* RESTATEMENT, 2D, PROPERTY (DONATIVE TRANSFERS) § 12.1, Comment g.
17. CAL. PROB. CODE § 267(b)(6) & (7) (West 2011).
18. TEX. PROB. CODE § 37A (Vernon's 2011).
19. N.Y. CLS EPTL § 2-1.11(b)(1) (McKinney's 2011).

4 FEDERAL TAX LAW OF PRE–1977 TRANSFERS

The law of disclaimers before the enactment of Section 2518 remains relevant because of the age of some existing estate planning documents, and the age of the potential disclaimants, discussed below.

A. Early Disclaimer Law

The first disclaimer law was a mess; after two early cases,[1] basic disclaimer law was set forth in Regs. Section 25.2511–1(c).[2] Further, Section 2055 recognized the

1. Hardenbergh v. Comr., 198 F.2d 63 (8th Cir. 1952), *cert. denied*, 344 U.S. 836 (1952); Brown v. Routzahn, 63 F.2d 914 (6th Cir. 1933), *rev'g* 58 F. Supp. 329 (N.D. Ohio 1931), *cert. denied*; 290 U.S. 641 (1933).

2. T.D. 6334, 1958-2 C.B. 627.

effectiveness of disclaimers for charitable bequests,[3] and early marital deduction law mentioned disclaimers.[4] Although these statutory provisions were repealed in 1976 when Section 2518 was enacted,[5] they still govern pre-1977 transfers.[6]

B. Law of Disclaimers of Pre–1977 Transfers

Treasury Regulation Section 25.2511–1(c)(2)[7] provides as follows:

- A disclaimer is a complete and unqualified refusal to accept the rights to which one is entitled;
- A refusal to accept ownership does not constitute a transfer;
- The refusal must be made within a reasonable time after learning of the transfer's existence;
- The refusal must be unequivocal and effective under local law. Where the local law does not permit such a refusal,

3. Section 2055(a), parenthetical clause in first sentence—"(including the interest which falls into any such [charitable] bequest, legacy, devise, or transfer as a result of an irrevocable disclaimer of a bequest, legacy, devise, transfer, or power, if the disclaimer is made before the date prescribed for the filing of the estate tax return)." This parenthetical clause was deleted by TRA 1976, § 2009(b)(4)(B), but it remains in § 2106(a)(2)(A).

4. § 2056(d)(1) (deleted by TRA 1976, § 2009(b)(4)(D)).

5. TRA 1976, Pub. L. No. 94–455, § 2009(b)(1). The complete release, or the lapse, of a general power of appointment created on or before October 21, 1942, is not deemed an exercise of that power. §§ 2041(a)(1), 2514(a). A disclaimer by operation of the facts of life for purposes of the estate tax charitable deduction still exists in § 2055(a), almost in the form quoted above.

6. The question of whether the timely disclaimer requirement of Regs. § 25.2511-1(c) applies to an interest created before November 14, 1958, the date of promulgation of the regulation, was raised by and decided against the taxpayer. Halbach Est. v. Comr., 71 T.C. 141 (1978).

7. *See also* Regs. §§ 20.2041-3(d)(6); 20.2055-2(c)(2); 20.2056(d) 1(a); 25.2514-2(c)(5). Sentences in this outline to which no footnotes are appended are to be found in Regs. § 25.2511-1(c).

any gratuitous transfer to another constitutes the making of a gift by that person;

- There can be no disclaimer after an acceptance of these rights, expressly or impliedly.[8]

If only a part of the property is refused, whether there has been a complete and unqualified refusal depends on the facts and circumstances, taking into account the effectiveness under the local law. If a disclaimer does not occur within a reasonable time after learning of the existence of the transfer, acceptance is presumed.

A disclaimer of a general power of appointment is not considered to be a lapse or release of the power, nor transfer of the property subject to the power.[9] If only a portion of the property subject to a power is disclaimed, whether or not there has been a complete and unqualified refusal will also depend on the facts and circumstances, taking into account local law.[10] Such rights refer to the incidents of the power and not to other interests of the decedent in the property. If effective under local law, the power may be disclaimed without disclaiming such other interests.[11] In the absence of facts to the contrary, the failure to disclaim within a reasonable time after learning of its existence will be presumed to constitute an acceptance of the power.[12]

---

8. Regs. § 20.2055-2(c)(2)(ii). *See also* PLR 7809043 (stepdaughter's disclaimer of her $4,000 income interest in a charitable trust, which does not presently qualify for the estate tax charitable deduction, in exchange for a lump sum equal to the cost of a $4,000 lifetime annuity is not a qualified disclaimer).

9. Regs. §§ 20.2041-3(d)(6); 25.2514-3(c)(5).

10. *Id.*

11. *Id.*

12. *Id.*

C. Case Law: Determining a "Reasonable Time"

The regulations allowed a disclaimer to be made within a reasonable time after learning of the transfer, which led to two additional questions: how long is a "reasonable time," and when does that time start? The resolution of these questions by the Eighth Circuit led to the enactment of Section 2518.

In *Keinath v. Comr.*,[13] the remainder beneficiary disclaimed his interest after the death of the income beneficiary, and almost 20 years after the creation of the trust. The tax court held that 19 years was not reasonable, but the Eighth Circuit reversed, holding that under state law the reasonable time period started on the death of the income beneficiary, not the grantor of the testamentary trust. The IRS refused to follow the decision,[14] even for taxpayers who could appeal to the Eighth Circuit.[15]

The applicability of *Keinath* was tested in the United States Supreme Court. In 1972 George Jewett disclaimed his remainder interest, then valued at $4 million, in a trust created for him under the will of his grandmother in 1939. As a result of conflicts between the circuits, Jewett took the case to the Supreme Court,[16] where he lost. The Supreme Court upheld the government's position that time to disclaim starts to run from the date of creation of the interest (or knowledge of creation of the interest), not from the date the interest vests or becomes possessory.

Two 1989 district court cases, relating to the same family, appeared to reopen *Keinath*;[17] but both were reversed, one by the

---

13. 480 F.2d 57 (8th Cir. 1973), *rev'g* 58 T.C. 352 (1972).

14. *See* PLR 7829008; PLR 7806080. *Cf.* PLR 7933066.

15. Cottrell v. Comr., 72 T.C. 489 (1979), *rev'd*, 628 F.2d 1127 (8th Cir. 1980).

16. 455 U.S. 305 (1982).

17. Ordway v. U.S., 89-1 USTC Para. 13,802 (S.D. Fla. 1989); Irvine v. U.S., 89-2 USTC Para.13,818 (D. Minn. 1989).

Supreme Court.[18] The facts in both cases were very similar; beneficiaries in 1979 disclaimed partial interests in trusts created in 1917, and the disclaimants had knowledge about the trusts since at least 1941. In similar opinions, two district courts held that neither disclaimant had made gifts because the disclaimers were timely. On appeal, one district court decision was reversed while the other was upheld,[19] but the government appealed to the Supreme Court. The Supreme Court, finding in favor of the government, held that, regardless of the application of Regs. Section 25.2511-1(c)(2), the general gift tax provisions caused the disclaimer to be a taxable gift. The Court rejected the disclaimant's reliance on state law, holding that "although state law creates legal interests and rights in property, federal law determines whether and to what extent those interests will be taxed."[20]

D. The Time Period: What Is a Reasonable Time?

As already discussed, Regs. Section 25.2511-1(c) applies to pre-1977 disclaimers. Unlike Section 2518, that regulation does not set a specific time period within which the disclaimer must be made. Instead, it provides that the disclaimer must be made "within a reasonable time after knowledge of the existence of the transfer." It can be hard to prove a lack of knowledge, however. For instance, a taxpayer asserted that in January 1985 he first learned of his contingent remainder interests in four trusts, each of which was cre-

18. The district court decision in *Ordway* was reversed in Ordway v. U.S., 908 F.2d 890 (11th Cir. 1990), *cert. denied*, 111 S. Ct. 2916 (1991). The Irvine decision was initially reversed in Irvine v. U.S., 936 F.2d 343 (8th Cir. 1991). However, the Eighth Circuit vacated its decision and granted an en banc rehearing, after which it affirmed the district court, 981 F.2d 991 (8th Cir. 1992). The en banc decision was then reversed by the Supreme Court, 114 S. Ct. 1473 (1994).

19. Irvine v. U.S., 936 F.2d 343 (8th Cir. 1991).

20. 511 U.S. 224 (1994).

ated before 1976, from the trustees of the trusts. The private letter ruling that he requested expressed no opinion with regard to the date on which the taxpayer first had knowledge of the existence of the contingent remainder interests in question.[21]

The Internal Revenue Service (IRS) has, however, issued a number of rulings finding that specific disclaimers were made within a reasonable time. In PLRs 9840007 and 9840009, the IRS permitted disclaimers of contingent income interests created in several trusts in 1958. The taxpayers disclaimed their interests within nine months after the decedent's death (in 1997), when the interests vested. The IRS stated that the interests were disclaimed within a reasonable time after the disclaimants obtained knowledge of the transfers creating the interests. The ruling notes that the taxpayers were not aware of the existence of the trusts until the decedent died.[22]

In PLR 200029048, the IRS accepted as timely a disclaimer where the decedent died before 1977, the decedent's grandson was one of the initial beneficiaries of the decedent's testamentary trust, and the grandson's son became a trust beneficiary when the grandson died. Within nine months of learning of the trust's existence at his father's death, the son disclaimed a fractional share of his interest in the trust's principal, while retaining the right to his share of the trust income and his remaining interest in the trust's principal.

In PLR 200109041, the IRS approved as timely a nephew's disclaimer of a percentage of the intestate share the nephew was entitled to receive from his uncle's estate. The uncle, who died before 1977, established a testamentary trust for his daughter. After the daughter's death, there was a dispute over whether the remain-

21. PLR 8601017. *See also* PLR 199934011 (decedent's spouse, who disclaimed her interest in the decedent's testamentary trust after the deaths of the initial beneficiaries, claimed that she made the disclaimer within nine months of learning of her rights in the trust; the IRS ruled that a disclaimer within nine months of learning of the existence of the trust would be timely but expressed "no opinion as to when [the spouse] first obtained the requisite knowledge of the transfer creating the interest").

22. The IRS approved similar disclaimers in PLRs 199945010, 199945012, 200040014, 200105049, and 200202036.

ing trust assets passed to the uncle's intestate heirs, including the nephew, or as appointed by the daughter's will. The daughter's will purported to appoint $100,000 of the trust assets to the nephew and the balance to a trust for a number of charities. Before receiving a letter from the attorney for the daughter's estate, the nephew had no knowledge of the provisions of the uncle's will or the daughter's will. The nephew entered into an agreement with the charities under which a portion of the trust was to be distributed among the uncle's intestate heirs and the balance was to be distributed to the daughter's appointees, excluding the nephew. The nephew also agreed to disclaim a percentage of the amount he was entitled to receive as an intestate heir of his uncle. The IRS ruled that the transfer creating the nephew's interest had occurred at the uncle's pre-1977 death and that the nephew made the disclaimer within a reasonable time of learning of the transfer creating his interest.

The regulations as to pre-1977 transfers provide nothing about a period of minority. Can knowledge not be presumed to exist until the person with the interest reaches a certain age or is competent? Is knowledge of the interest on the part of the guardian or conservator of an underage or incompetent ward imputed to the ward? In the private letter rulings that have dealt with disclaimers of pre-1977 transfers, after the period of minority ends, the disclaimants have used Section 2518 as a safe harbor and attempted to keep within the time period prescribed therein.[23]

In PLR 9413026, the IRS approved a disclaimer of a pre-1977 interest made within nine months of the disclaimant's reaching age 18 (the state law age of majority), stating that nine months is usually deemed to be a reasonable time. Similarly, in PLRs 200238039 and 200240015, the IRS ruled that disclaimers of contingent future interests in pre-1977 trusts made within nine months of the disclaimants' reaching age 18 (the applicable age of majority) would be considered made within the time prescribed in Section 25.2511-1(c). In all three of these private rulings, the IRS cited *Jewett* for the proposition that the time limitation for making a disclaimer does not begin to run until the disclaimant attains the age of majority.

23. PLRs 8825101, 8638022, 8351120, 8246041, 8205066 (correcting 8151130), and 8045093.

FEDERAL TAX LAW OF THE QUALIFIED DISCLAIMER—SECTION 2518

5

The disclaimer landscape changed dramatically with the passage of Section 2518, which applies to post-1976 transfers. When most practitioners talk about disclaimers, it is usually with an eye to this body of law.

A. GENERALLY

Section 2518, which implemented to concept of a "qualified disclaimer" for transfer tax purposes, was enacted to overrule *Keinath*. The qualified disclaimer rules apply to post-1976 transfers creating an interest in the disclaimant.[1] A qualified disclaimer is an irrevocable and unqualified refusal to accept an interest, or undivided portion of an interest, in property.[2] An interest in property includes a power with respect to

1. Pub. L. No. 94-455, § 2009(e)(2); Regs. § 25.2518-1(a)(1).
2. § 2518(b), (c)(1); Regs. §§ 25.2518-2(a)(1), -3(a)(1)(i).

the property.[3] The effect of a qualified disclaimer is that no transfer is deemed to have been made to or from the person making the disclaimer.[4] The refusal must be in writing,[5] identifying the interest in property disclaimed, signed by the disclaimant or the disclaimant's legal representative,[6] and delivered to[7] the transferor of the interest, the transferor's legal representative, or the holder of the legal title to the property to which the interest relates,[8] no later than nine months after the date of the transfer creating the interest, or nine months after the disclaimant becomes 21.[9] The disclaimant must not have accepted the interest or any of its benefits.[10] As a result of the disclaimer, the interest must pass, without any direction on the part of the disclaimant, either to the spouse

3. § 2518(c)(2); Regs. § 25.2518-3(a)(1)(iii).

4. § 2518(a); Regs. § 25.2518-1(b).

5. § 2518(b)(1); Regs. § 25.2518-2(a)(2), (b)(1). *See* TAM 9640005 (ledger, probate inventory, and unsigned letter from attorney submitted in support of contention that decedent made a § 2518 qualified disclaimer before his death fail to meet § 2518 requirement of a written instrument showing irrevocable and unqualified refusal to accept property).

6. Regs. § 25.2518-2(b)(1). The term *legal representative* is not defined. It should include any agent designated by the disclaimant and any court-appointed fiduciary for the disclaimant or the disclaimant's estate. State law and the disclaimant's grant of authority govern the issue of the agent's or fiduciary's authority to disclaim. In Delaune Est. v. U.S., 143 F.3d 995 (5th Cir. 1998), *rev'g* Barman Est. v. U.S., 97-1 USTC ¶ 60,266 (M.D. La. 1997), *cert. denied*, 525 U.S. 1072 (1999), the heirs of a Louisiana decedent successfully disclaimed on the decedent's behalf a portion of the inheritance the decedent received from her predeceased husband because Louisiana allows the renunciation of a succession by the heirs of an heir on the heir's behalf.

7. § 2518(b)(2) ("received by"); Regs. § 25.2518-2(b)(2) ("delivered to"). Regs. § 25.2518-2(c)(2) states that timely mailing is timely delivery if the mailing requirements of the pertinent provisions of Regs. § 301.7502-1 are met; and that the first day following a Saturday, Sunday, or legal holiday is the due date, by reference to Regs. § 301.7503-1.

8. *See, e.g.*, PLRs 9016026 and 9017026.

9. § 2518(b)(2); Regs. § 25.2518-2(c)(1).

10. § 2518(b)(3); Regs. § 25.2518-2(d).

of the transferor[11] or to a person other than the disclaimant.[12] These requirements are discussed separately, below.

B. REQUIREMENTS FOR A DISCLAIMER: THE FIVE TESTS

As noted above, a disclaimer is "qualified" if it meets four statutory tests.[13] First, it must be in a writing that adequately describes the disclaimed property (the "writing test"). Second, it must be received by the transferor, her legal representative, or the holder of legal title to property no later than nine months after the later of (1) the date on which the transfer creating the interest in the disclaimant is made; or (2) the date on which the disclaimant turns 21 (the "nine-month test"). Third, the disclaimant must not have accepted the property or any benefits from it (the "no-benefit test"). Fourth, the property must pass, without direction from the disclaimant, to either (1) the transferor's spouse; or (2) a person other than the disclaimant (the "passage test"). In addition to these four statutory tests, the disclaimer probably has to meet the state law test of validity. Each of these tests is discussed below.

1. WRITING TEST

The writing test is the easiest to satisfy. Among other things, the writing should (1) state the disclaimant's irrevocable and unqualified refusal to accept the interest in property to be disclaimed; (2) adequately describe that interest; and (3) include a date and an acknowledgment of receipt. Not all writings are sufficient. In a tax court case,[14] a disclaimer failed in part because the writing did not properly identify the assets being disclaimed. The only

11. § 2518(b)(4)(A), as amended by Pub. L. No. 95-600, § 700(m); Regs. § 25.2518-2(e)(2).
12. § 2518(b)(4)(B); Regs. § 25.2518-2(e)(1).
13. CODE § 2518(b).
14. Chamberlain v. Commissioner, T.C.M. 1999-181; this case was affirmed by the Ninth Circuit in an unpublished opinion, Chamberlain v. Commissioner, 87 AFTR 2d 2001–2386.

written documents available were a list of the deceased transferor's assets (essentially an informal inventory), together with a document the disclaimant intended to sign (but did not) that stated a specific amount to be disclaimed but that failed to identify particular assets.

2. Nine-Month Test

Section 2518(b)(2) requires that the disclaimer, which must be in writing, must be "received. . . not later than the date which is 9 months after" the later of the date of the taxable transfer or the disclaimant's twenty-first birthday. The consequences of missing this date can be unfortunate. For instance, in *Fleming Est. v. Comr.*,[15] an executor disclaimed a second decedent's interest in the estate of the first decedent. The executor counted the nine-month disclaimer period as starting not from the date of death of the first decedent but from the date that the decedent's will was probated. The executor and his lawyer looked at the term *transfer* in Section 2518, but not at the Section 2518 regulations, and decided that under state law the transfer of an interest in personal property by will occurs on the date the will is admitted to probate.

Further, in TAM 8730004, the marital deduction was lost for the wife's life estate in a $9,700,000 charitable remainder unitrust under her deceased husband's will because the husband's brother, the contingent beneficiary of the secondary life estate, sought to disclaim his life estate after nine months from the date of the husband's death. The wife was 59 years old, and the brother was 83 years old. Therefore, it was extremely unlikely that the brother would survive the wife. In addition, it appeared that the brother had no need for the contingent life estate. From facts given in the ruling, it appeared as if the brother were as wealthy as his deceased brother.

To meet this test, one must know how the nine months is determined, what constitutes receipt, when did the transfer occur that starts the clock running, and how minors are treated.

---

15. 58 T.C.M. 1034 (1989), *aff'd*, 974 F.2d 894, 92-2 USTC Para. 60,113 (7th Cir. 1992).

A. Receipt, Recipient, and Delivery

Section 2518(b)(2) requires that the written disclaimer be "received by the transferor of the [disclaimed] interest, his legal representative, or the holder of the legal title to the property to which the [disclaimed] interest relates." Therefore, trust beneficiaries can deliver disclaimers either to the settlor or to the trustee. The disclaimant of life insurance proceeds should be able to deliver the disclaimer either to the representative of the insured's estate or to the insurance company, and a surviving joint tenant should be able to deliver it either to the representative of the deceased joint tenant's estate or to the bank.[16] In the latter two situations, however, prudence dictates that both parties receive the disclaimer.

Receipt by a third person can prove the timeliness of the disclaimer, but if the disclaimant of an interest in an estate is also the sole executor of that estate, receipt by the disclaimant of her own written disclaimer should be sufficient if allowed under local law. In *Hankins Est. v. Comr.*,[17] the decedent devised a life estate in real property to his wife, with remainder to his son, and named the son as executor. Although the son gave timely notice to his mother of his disclaimer of his remainder interest, it was ineffective because the son failed to file it with the local probate court, as state law required. If there had been no filing requirement, the disclaimer would have been effective because the son, as executor, was the person required to have received his own disclaimer.

Treasury Regulation Section 25.2518-2(b)(2) treats "receipt" as delivery, and Regs. Section 25.2518-2(c)(2) provides that a disclaimer that is timely mailed (as defined under Section 7502 and its regulations) is timely delivered. Under Section 7502, the postmark governs, use of registered or certified mail secures the date and provides evidence of delivery, and designated private delivery services can be used.

16. *See, e.g.*, PLRs 9016026 and 9017026.
17. 42 T.C.M. 229 (1981).

B. The Period: Nine Months

Under Section 2518, the disclaimer period ends "not later than the date which is 9 months after the date on which the transfer creating the interest"[18] is made. Lack of knowledge of the interest does not extend that period, nor is an extension allowed if, for instance, an interest in an estate is being disclaimed, and an extension of time for filing the estate tax return is obtained, or if a request for a private letter ruling is pending.[19] However, Regs. Section 25.2518-2(c)(2) does permit an extension to the next succeeding day if the last day of the period falls on Saturday, Sunday, or a legal holiday.

C. Starting Point: The Transfer Creating the Interest

Under Section 2518(b)(2)(A), the date of the "transfer creating the interest" is the starting point for the nine-month period. No transfer tax need be imposed on the transfer for it to be subject to the disclaimer rules.[20] For example, Regs. Section 25.2518-2(c)(3)(i) provides that a bequest of foreign situs property by a nonresident alien decedent is a transfer creating the interest even if the transfer is not subject to estate tax.

The Section 2518(b)(2)(A) starting point, "the date on which the transfer creating the interest in. . . [the disclaimant] is made," can change, depending on the type of transfer. It can occur when there is a completed transfer for gift tax purposes (whether or not a gift tax is imposed), or upon the date of the decedent's death with respect to testamentary transfers.[21] So, for example, if the transfer

18. § 2518(b)(2); Regs. § 25.2518-2(c)(1). The IRS, in a Notice or other guidance, may provide for the postponement of the deadline for making the disclaimer for members of the Armed Forces serving in a combat zone (§ 7508) or for taxpayers affected by a presidentially declared disaster (§ 7508A). Rev. Proc. 2002-71, 2002-46 I.R.B. 850, § 9.17. *See, e.g.*, Notice 2001-68, 2001-47 I.R.B. 504 (terrorist attacks of Sept. 11, 2001).

19. *See, e.g.*, Fitzgerald v. U.S., 94–1 USTC Para. 60,152 (W.D. La. 1993), in which an estate unsuccessfully argued that an extension of the time in which to file the estate tax return also extended the nine-month disclaimer period.

20. *See* REG-208215-91, 61 Fed. Reg. 43197 (8/21/96), Preamble; T.D. 8744, 62 Fed. Reg. 68183 (12/31/97), Preamble.

21. Regs. § 25.2518-2(c)(3). *See* H.R. Rep. No. 94-1380, at 67 (1976).

is for the life of an income beneficiary with a remainder interest to another, both parties (whether their interests are vested or contingent) must disclaim within nine months of the original transfer.[22]

(1) Lifetime Trust Transfers

The starting point for a beneficiary's disclaiming trust interests created during the grantor's lifetime is the date the property is transferred to the trust, *regardless* of the type of interest the beneficiary holds. If O creates an irrevocable inter vivos trust on April 1, 1978, with income payable to O's child D for life and remainder at D's death to D's child, E, the starting point for D's and E's disclaimers is April 1, 1978.[23] If subsequent additions are made to such a trust, the disclaimer starting point is the date of the addition to the trust.[24]

If a husband and wife reside in a community property state and on April 1, 1978, they purchase real property with community funds and do not put the real property in their names as joint tenants with right of survivorship, and the husband dies on January 3, 1985, devising his position of the property to the wife, the wife can disclaim that portion within nine months of the husband's death but cannot disclaim the interest in the property that she acquired on April 1, 1978.[25]

(2) Revocable Transfers: Joint Accounts, Totten Trusts, and Others

Certain transfers are revocable. These include not only transfers to revocable trusts, but also to joint accounts, Totten trusts, and others. The starting point for the disclaimer period varies depending upon the type of interest involved. For example, in the case of revocable trusts, the disclaimer period does not begin on the date the trust is created, but rather on the date of each distribution (which is usually the date of the grantor's death, when the interests involved are remainder interests).[26]

---

22. Regs. § 25.2518-2(c)(3).
23. Regs. § 25.2518-2(c)(5), Ex. 3.
24. *See, e.g.*, PLR 9210014.
25. Regs. § 25.2518-2(c)(5), Ex. 11.
26. Regs. § 25.2518-2(c)(5), Ex. 6.

In the case of joint bank accounts, if B transfers all of the assets to a bank account that is held jointly by B and C, the starting point for C's disclaimer of the bank account is the date of B's death, because until that time B could have withdrawn all the funds and therefore the transfer was not complete.[27] This same rule, that the date of the contributor's death starts the disclaimer period, applies to jointly held certificates of deposit, savings certificates, investment accounts, or "nominally titled joint brokerage accounts";[28] the so-called "Totten Trust";[29] and jointly held "cash management accounts" at a brokerage firm.[30] The disclaimer period for life insurance proceeds payable to someone other than the policy owner is the date of the insured's death.[31]

(3) Powers of Appointment

There are several variables with powers of appointment. First, is the disclaimer being considered a disclaimer of the power itself, or a gift under the power? If the latter, is it a gift under a general or a limited power? A general power of appointment, of course, is a power to dispose of property, created by someone other than the power holder, that can be exercised in favor of the power holder, her estate, her creditors, or the creditors of her estate. A limited or nongeneral power, on the other hand, can be exercised in favor of anyone *except* the holder, her estate, her creditors, or the creditors of her estate.[32] A power limited by "an ascertainable standard," even if to the holder herself, is not a general power;[33] nor is a power exercisable only in conjunction with the creator of the

---

27. Regs. § 25.2518-2(c)(5), Ex. 12.
28. *See, e.g.*, PLRs 8916070, 8904041, 8728012, and 8648070.
29. PLR 8648070.
30. PLRs 9113011, 8827072. *But see* PLR 8609083 (stock transferred by decedent to jointly held cash management account must be disclaimed within 9 months of date of that transfer).
31. PLR 8702024.
32. §§ 2041(b)(1), 2514(c).
33. §§ 2041(b)(1)(A), 2514(c)(1).

power or with a person with a substantial adverse interest in the property subject to the power.[34]

The disclaimer starting point is postponed to the power holder's death in the case of a general power;[35] but for limited powers, it is the date the power is created. For example, on May 13, 1978, B creates a trust in which C is given a lifetime income interest and a general power of appointment over the principal. C exercises the general power of appointment in favor of D upon C's death on June 17, 1989. The starting point for a disclaimer by D is June 17, 1989.[36] So, paradoxically, the disclaimer period for possible appointees under a general power starts on the exercise or lapse of the power, but the disclaimer period for potential appointees under a broad limited power of appointment (which is not much different) starts upon the creation of the trust creating the limited power.

The starting point for disclaimers of the powers themselves, by comparison, is the same, whether they are general or limited powers: the date of the creation of the power.[37]

Finally, for powers of appointment established before October 22, 1942, the time to disclaim runs from the exercise, lapse, or release.[38]

(4) Lifetime Transfers That Are Includable in the Transferor's Estate

If a transfer creating an interest is subject to federal gift tax, and that interest is later included in the transferor's gross estate for federal estate tax purposes, the disclaimer period starts to run on the date of the gift, not inclusion in the estate.[39] This may occur

34. §§ 2041(b)(1)(C), 2514(c)(3). A power "exercisable by the decedent [possessor] only in conjunction with another person" is not a general power if created on or before Oct. 21, 1942. §§ 2041(b)(1)(B), 2514(c)(2).

35. Regs. § 25.2518-2(c)(3), (c)(5), Ex. 2. *See, e.g.*, PLR 9340052.

36. *See* Regs. § 25.2518-2(c)(5), Exs. 1 and 2.

37. Regs. § 25.2518-2(c)(3)(i).

38. *See* Regs. § 25.2518-2(c)(3)(i).

39. Regs. § 25.2518-2(c)(3).

with transfers subject to Section 2035 (the "three-year rule"),[40] or with transfers with retained interests (for example, if a transferor retains voting rights in transferred stock, the disclaimer period is not postponed to the settlor's death even though the retained right causes estate tax inclusion).[41]

(5) Qualified Terminable Interest Property and Qualified Domestic Trust

The date of the first spouse's death is the starting point for the disclaimer period for a current or remainder beneficiary of a qualified terminable interest property (QTIP) trust, just as with any other trust. The fact that the trust property is includable in the surviving spouse's estate has no effect on that result. So, for example, in the case of a remainder interest in property which an executor elects to treat as QTIP under Section 2056(b)(7), the remainderman must disclaim within nine months of the transfer creating the interest, rather than nine months from the date such interest is subject to tax under Section 2044 or Section 2519.[42]

Further, the time within which a remainderman of a qualified domestic trust (QDT)[43] can disclaim his interest runs from date of the deceased spouse's death. Presumably, if the surviving spouse is a U.S. resident and is given a general power of appointment in the QDT, the starting point for a remainderman's disclaimer is the exercise or lapse of that power.[44]

---

40. Section 2035 provides that the only inter vivos transfers included in a decedent's gross estate by virtue of being made within three years of the date of death are transfers of interests in property includible in the decedent's gross estate under § 2036, § 2037, § 2038, or § 2042 or that would have been included under any of these sections if the interest transferred had instead been retained by the decedent.

41. § 2036(a) and (b).

42. Regs. § 25.2518-2(c)(3).

43. For the disallowance of the estate tax marital deduction where the surviving spouse is not a U.S. citizen, unless the decedent's property passes to a QDT, *see* §§ 2056(d), 2056A.

44. *See* Regs. § 25.2518-2(c)(3).

(6) Successive Disclaimers

More than one disclaimer may be required for the disclaimed property to fall into the hands of the right person. In this case, all disclaimers must be made within the same nine-month period. A person who receives an interest in property as the result of a qualified disclaimer of the interest must "disclaim the previously disclaimed interest no later than nine months after the date of the taxable transfer creating the interest in the preceding disclaimant."[45]

For instance, assume wife dies intestate, is survived by a husband and three adult daughters, and that under the state laws of intestacy, husband is only entitled to one-fourth of the intestate estate. If the daughters wanted their father to receive the entire estate, not only would each have to disclaim her intestate share, but so would any of their children (husband's grandchildren). The disclaimers by the daughters and the grandchildren must be made within nine months of the wife's death.

(7) Joint Property

The history of disclaimers of jointly held interests is rather tortured but was largely resolved with final regulations in 1997. Those regulations distinguish between the disclaimer of jointly held bank, brokerage, or investment accounts and the disclaimer of other jointly held property.

(a) Property Other Than Bank and Investment Accounts

Under the regulations,[46] tenancies that are unilaterally severable are treated the same as those that are not (e.g., tenancies by the entirety). A surviving joint tenant may disclaim the one-half survivorship interest in property held in a joint tenancy with right of survivorship or a tenancy by the entirety (except for joint bank, brokerage, and investment accounts)[47] within nine months of the date of death of the first joint tenant to die, whether or not the

45. Regs. § 25.2518-2(c)(3)(i).
46. T.D. 8744, 62 Fed. Reg. 68183 (12/31/97).
47. Addressed in Regs. § 25.2518-2(c)(4)(iii).

interest can be unilaterally severed under local law. The disclaimed interest is deemed to be a one-half interest in the property, regardless of the property attributable to the consideration furnished by the disclaimant and the portion of the property included in the decedent's gross estate.[48]

The regulations retain the rule for both types of tenancies requiring a disclaimer of the interest to which the disclaimant succeeds upon creation of the tenancy to be made within nine months after the creation of the tenancy.[49] So, for example, assume that on February 1, 1990, B purchased real property with B's funds, acquiring title as "B and C, as joint tenants with right of survivorship." Under applicable state law, the joint interest is unilaterally severable by either tenant. C dies on May 1, 1998, survived by B. On January 1, 1999, B disclaims the one-half survivorship interest in the property to which B succeeds as a result of C's death. B has made a qualified disclaimer of the one-half survivorship interest (but not the interest retained by B upon the creation of the tenancy, which may not be disclaimed by B). The result is the same whether or not B and C are married and regardless of the proportion of consideration furnished by B and C in purchasing the property. The result also is the same if B and C held the property as tenants by the entirety in a state that does not allow unilateral severance by either tenant.[50]

The regulations also provide that continued occupancy of a residence by the surviving joint tenant after disclaiming the one-half survivorship interest does not cause the survivor to be deemed to have accepted the interest or any of its benefits, because occupancy after the joint owner's death is consistent with the survivor's retained undivided ownership interest.[51]

The regulations[52] retain the special rule for tenancies created on or after July 14, 1988, to which Section 2523(i)(3) applies (i.e., the donor's spouse is not a U.S. citizen). Thus, the surviving spouse

48. Under § 2040.
49. Regs. § 25.2518-2(c)(4)(i).
50. *See* Regs. § 25.2518-2(c)(5), Exs. 7 and 8.
51. *See* Regs. § 25.2518-2(c)(5), Ex. 10.
52. Regs. § 25.2518-2(c)(4)(ii).

may disclaim any portion of the joint interest that is includible in the decedent-donor's gross estate.[53]

Example: On March 1, 1989, H and W purchase vacant land that is conveyed to them as tenants by the entirety. The entire consideration is paid by H. W is not a U.S. citizen. H dies on June 1, 1998. W can disclaim the entire joint interest because this is the interest includible in H's gross estate.[54] Assuming that the executor of H's estate receives W's disclaimer no later than nine months after June 1, 1998, W's disclaimer of the property would be a qualified disclaimer. The result would be the same if the property was held in joint tenancy with right of survivorship that was unilaterally severable under local law.[55]

(B) Bank, Brokerage, and Investment Accounts

In the case of jointly held bank, brokerage, or investment accounts, if the creation of an account is not a completed gift,[56] the regulations require the surviving joint tenant to disclaim within nine months of the death of the contributing joint tenant.[57] No portion of the disclaimant's contributions may be disclaimed, even if only one-half of the property is included in the decedent's gross estate under the joint property rules.[58] This rule applies to both spousal and nonspousal joint tenancies.

This rule can lead to differing results. Assume that, on July 1, 1990, B contributes $50,000 to open a bank account held jointly with C, B's spouse. C contributes nothing. Because B can withdraw all the cash in the account without C's consent, the transfer is not a completed gift.[59] If B dies on August 15, 1998, and C disclaims the entire amount in the bank account on October 15 of that year, the disclaimer is qualified because it was made within nine months after B's death. The disclaimed account balance passes through

53. Under § 2040.
54. Under § 2040(a).
55. *See* Regs. § 25.2518-2(c)(5), Ex. 9.
56. Under Regs. § 25.2511-1(h)(4).
57. Regs. § 25.2518-2(c)(4)(iii).
58. § 2040(b).
59. Under Regs. § 25.2511-1(h)(4).

B's probate estate and is no longer joint property includible in B's gross estate.[60] Instead, the entire account is includible in B's gross estate as property in which B retained an interest.[61] If instead C had died first, B would not be able to disclaim any of the funds in the bank account, because B furnished the funds for the entire account and did not relinquish dominion and control over the funds. The above results would be the same if B and C were not married.[62]

On the other hand, if C had disclaimed 40 percent of the funds in the account, that disclaimed portion would no longer be characterized as joint property and would be includible in B's gross estate,[63] while the remaining 60 percent of the account balance would be includible in B's gross estate because it retains its character as joint property.[64] In this case, the result changes, depending on marital status. If B and C were married, B's gross estate would include 30 percent (1/2 × 60 percent) of the account balance,[65] and 70 percent of the aggregate balance. If B and C were not married, then the 40 percent disclaimed portion would be includible in B's gross estate[66] as property in which B retained an interest, and the remaining 60 percent would be includible in B's gross estate[67] because B furnished all of the funds with respect to the account.[68]

(8) COMMUNITY PROPERTY

The rules for disclaimers of community property are simpler, because the deceased spouse's death is always the starting point for the surviving spouse's disclaimer of the deceased spouse's half of the community property.[69]

---

60. Under § 2040.
61. Under § 2033.
62. *See* Regs. § 25.2518-2(c)(5), Exs. 12 and 13.
63. Under § 2033.
64. § 2040.
65. Under § 2040(b).
66. Under § 2033.
67. Under § 2040(a).
68. *See* Regs. § 25.2518-2(c)(5), Ex. 14.
69. Regs. § 25.2518-2(c)(5), Ex. 10. *See also* PLR 9507017 (disclaimer time period runs from death of first spouse to die for property passing under Washington community property agreement).

(9) The Period: The Age 21 Stretch Out

Minors (for federal tax law disclaimer purposes, those under age 21)[70] are not subject to the nine-month rule. Under the regulations, for example,[71] assume that in 1979, D established a trust for the benefit of D's minor children, E and F. Under the terms of the trust, the trustee can make discretionary distributions of income and principal to both children, and the trust property is divided equally between them when E reaches age 35. Before reaching age 21 years on April 8, 1982, E receives several trust income distributions. After reaching that age, E receives no further distributions. Four months later, E disclaims all interest in trust income, so that all income will be distributed to F. If the remaining requirements of Section 2518 are met, E's disclaimer is a qualified disclaimer under Section 2518(a). However, if E had accepted trust income within the four months between E's twenty-first birthday and the disclaimer date, the disclaimer would not have been qualified.

In another example, assume that F gives shares of stock to G as custodian for H, who is 15 at the time of the gift, under the local Uniform Gifts to Minors Act. H receives the shares outright from G when he reaches age 18. After receiving the shares and before H's twenty-first birthday, H receives dividends. If, within 9 months of reaching age 21, H disclaims the 10 shares, and if H does not accept any dividends after turning 21, the disclaimer is qualified.

This delay of the time for a disclaimer can lead to conflicts with other transfer tax provisions. For example, can an estate obtain the benefit of an estate tax marital or charitable deduction on account of a qualified disclaimer made by a minor's guardian within nine months of the decedent's death but revoked years later upon the minor's twenty-first birthday? Or does it mean that the availability of a marital or charitable deduction is a question to be held open until nine months after the minor's twenty-first birthday? Several letter rulings have acknowledged the effectiveness, for

70. Regs. § 25.2518-2(d)(3) provides that actions taken with regard to a property interest by a beneficiary or a custodian prior to the beneficiary's twenty-first birthday will not be an acceptance by the beneficiary of the interest.

71. Regs. § 25.2518-2(d)(4).

marital deduction purposes, of court-approved disclaimers executed by guardians of minors within nine months of the taxable transfer creating the disclaimed interest.[72] The question of whether these disclaimers could be revoked at some time in the future has not been raised.

There is also the question of whether the Internal Revenue Service (IRS) will recognize a disclaimer made by a minor when it appears to be contrary to state law. The IRS challenged court-approved disclaimers on behalf of a decedent's minor children in *Goree Est. v. Comr.*,[73] arguing that the disclaimers were not valid under local (Alabama) law because they were not in the best interests of the children. The children disclaimed their interests to their mother, the surviving spouse, to qualify the property for the marital deduction. The IRS argued that the surviving spouse, as the children's conservator, made the disclaimers solely to avoid federal estate tax and benefit the decedent's estate. The tax court, however, held that the disclaimers were qualified, finding that preservation of the decedent's estate to provide for the children was a valid reason for disclaimer under Alabama law. The IRS later issued a nonacquiescence.[74]

3. No Benefits (or No Acceptance) Test

The regulations provide that a "qualified disclaimer cannot be made with respect to any interest in property if the disclaimant has accepted the interest or any of its benefits, expressly or impliedly, prior to making the disclaimer."[75] Acts of acceptance include using disclaimed property; accepting dividends, rents, or interest from

72. *See, e.g.*, PLR 9051007 (disclaimer by adult children of trust interests, with backup disclaimer by guardian ad litem, with court approval, of minor grandchildren's interests in trust, produced an intestate share for surviving spouse that qualified for the marital deduction); TAM 9003007 (disclaimer of benefit of discretionary distributions of income and principal from trust by adult children and guardian ad litem for minor grandchildren and unborn and unascertained contingent beneficiaries qualified trust for QTIP election).

73. T.C. Memo 1994-331, *nonacq.*, 1996-2 C.B. 1.

74. AOD 1996–001.

75. Regs. § 25.2518-2(d)(1).

the property; or directing others to act with respect to the property (unless the disclaimant is under age 21). Further, the acceptance of any consideration in return for making the disclaimer is an acceptance of the benefits of the entire interest disclaimed.[76] Further, withdrawal of funds from a joint account, even if the withdrawal is accidental and the funds are later returned, amounts to acceptance.[77] On the other hand, merely acting as a fiduciary with respect to the property is not acceptance of a benefit, *unless* the fiduciary has the power to direct where the property is to go.[78]

There are two lines of "acceptance" cases: those determined solely under state law, and those determined for federal transfer tax purposes (which include IRS pronouncements). What follows is the federal line of cases only; the state law cases are discussed later in this volume.

A. Findings of No Acceptance

Two Fifth Circuit "acceptance" cases are taxpayer friendly. In the first,[79] the court held that the heirs of a surviving spouse could disclaim on her behalf property of the predeceased spouse. The disclaimed property was held in a single community property account, from which the surviving spouse's son continued to pay her expenses and to which he transferred cash on one occasion. The court ruled that it was not consistent with ownership of the predeceased spouse's property for the surviving spouse to pay her own expenses from joint funds to which she had an equal right, nor was it an affirmative act for her to passively accept "routine interest accrual."

The second case,[80] even more favorable, held that implied promises to disclaimants that they would be better off if they disclaimed property did not amount to coercion or compensation for disclaiming. The court held that a mere "expectation of a future benefit in return for executing a disclaimer" will not render the

76. Treas. Reg. § 25-2518-2(d)(4), Ex. 2.
77. PLR 9012053 (*but see* DeLaune, below).
78. Treas. Reg. § 25.2518-2(d).
79. DeLaune v. U.S., 143 F.3d 995 (5th Cir. 1998).
80. Monroe v. Commissioner, 124 F.3d 699 (5th Cir. 1997).

disclaimer unqualified. The court refused to find consideration for the disclaimers or to apply the step-transaction or substance-over-form theory to find consideration.

In PLR 9319022 there was a disclaimer of a bequest of stock under a decedent's will. Even though the disclaimant was a co-trustee of the charitable trust to which the disclaimed stock passed, he was ruled not to have accepted any benefits of the stock, since the other trustee established a charitable corporation to receive the disclaimed stock. The disclaimant also timely disclaimed all his right to (1) serve as a trustee of the charitable trust; (2) appoint a successor trustee of the charitable trust; and (3) serve in any position with any entity established by the trustee of the charitable trust that will receive the stock he disclaimed. The IRS ruled that the disclaimant could still serve as an officer, director, member of the grants committee, or in other capacities with respect to the charitable corporation that held the retained stock, since that corporation will never hold any of the disclaimed stock.

If one interest in property is accepted, it will not necessarily taint the disclaimer of another separate interest in the same property.[81] So, for example, if beneficiary is entitled to trust income and, at age 30, the principal, and beneficiary receives an income distribution before age 30, the disclaimer of the income interest would not be not a qualified, but a disclaimer of the principal might be.[82] Further, where a beneficiary disclaimed a fractional share of a trust, her receipt of the pro rata share of trust income allocable to the nondisclaimed share of the trust was not an acceptance.[83]

81. Regs. § 25.2518-2(d)(1).

82. Regs. § 25.2518-2(d)(4), Ex. 1. *But see* Regs. § 25.2518-3(d), Ex. 18 (where A bequeathed his residuary estate outright and not in trust to B, distribution of all of the income of the estate to B precludes B's disclaimer of any portion of the residuary estate). *See also* Walshire Est. v. U.S., 288 F.3d 342 (8th Cir. 2002) (taxpayer's acceptance of income from an outright bequest precluded valid disclaimer of the remainder interest; the taxpayer accepted benefit of the remainder interest because, without the principal, there would have been no income).

83. PLR 8637113. *See also* PLR 9008034, TAM 8619002, and PLR 8729008.

The regulations' examples of no acceptance are generous:

- If a disclaimant is both a beneficiary and a fiduciary, the exercise of fiduciary powers to preserve or maintain the disclaimed property is not treated as an acceptance of the disclaimed property or of any of its benefits.[84]
- A joint tenant in residential real property is not considered to have accepted the joint interest merely because he resides on the property before disclaiming his interest in it.[85] If the disclaimant retains her own half of the property and disclaims the share from a deceased joint tenant, neither her continued occupancy of the house before her disclaimer nor the fact that she lives in the residence after her disclaimer disqualifies her disclaimer.[86]
- Merely paying the property taxes does not constitute acceptance even if the disclaimant's personal funds were used to pay them.[87]
- State law's required use of a quitclaim deed to effectuate a disclaimer of real property does not constitute acceptance that would disqualify an otherwise qualified disclaimer.[88] The regulations state that "merely taking delivery of an instrument of title, without more, does not constitute acceptance. Moreover, a disclaimant is not considered to have accepted property merely because under applicable local law title to the property vests immediately in the disclaimant upon the death of a decedent."[89]
- If a decedent's stock is deposited in an account held jointly by the disclaimant and the decedent without the

---

84. Regs. § 25.2518-2(d)(2). *See also* PLR 8922082.
85. Regs. § 25.2518-2(d)(1). *See also* PLR 9135043.
86. Regs. § 25.2518-2(d)(4), Ex. 8. *Accord* PLR 9507017.
87. *Compare* Regs. § 25.2518-2(d)(4), Ex. 3 *with* Prop. Regs. § 25.2518-2(d)(1)(iii), Ex. 3 (which were not adopted). *See* PLR 9135043 (payment of mortgage principal and interest, real estate taxes, and other expenses related to the residence are not acceptance since they are a natural consequence of the use and occupancy of the residence.)
88. Regs. § 25.2518-1(c)(1)(i).
89. Regs. § 25.2518-2(d)(1).

disclaimant's knowledge, the disclaimant may make a qualified disclaimer of the stock.[90]

- A surviving spouse's retitling of bank and brokerage accounts held as community property to her sole name for income tax purposes was not an acceptance of the decedent's community property interest.[91]
- A surviving spouse who, at the request of the brokerage firm, transfers the entire assets in a joint tenancy account to an account held solely in husband's name, but who deposits half the securities in a separate account for the wife's estate upon becoming executor, can make a qualified disclaimer over the deceased spouse's one-half interest.[92]
- Amendment of a trust that holds disclaimed property simply to appoint a trustee does not amount to acceptance.[93]

Voting to amend a limited liability company (LLC) agreement does not amount to an acceptance of an interest in the LLC, at least where the vote is made in the disclaimant's fiduciary capacity (as personal representative of the decedent's estate) and not in the disclaimant's individual capacity.[94]

B. Findings of Acceptance

Acceptance of property to be disclaimed can occur by accepting a benefit from the property itself, or by receiving consideration for the disclaimer. In fact, it need not even involve receiving a "benefit" at all; simply behaving as though the disclaimant owned the property can be enough. For instance, in PLR 8702024, the decedent's sister, beneficiary of the decedent's group life insurance policy, sought to disclaim half of the proceeds so that they would pass by intestacy to the decedent's daughter. However, the decedent's employer had forwarded a claim form to the sister that she

90. TAM 9243024.

91. PLR 9507017.

92. PLR 199932042. *See also* PLR 200503024 (simply changing the title to the brokerage account did not constitute acceptance, and withdrawal of cash from an account and directing sale of certain assets did not prevent disclaiming other assets).

93. PLR 200443030.

94. PLR 200406038.

then promptly forwarded to the insurance company with proof of the insured's death. The insurance company then established an account in the sister's name and sent her checks on the account. The sister's subsequent proposal to disclaim, though well within the nine-month period of Section 2518 and before any drawing on the account by her, was held disqualified because of her acts of acceptance—her "affirmative acts with respect to the proceeds of X's life insurance policy that were consistent with ownership."

Another example of acceptance is *Selby Est. v. U.S.*[95] The mother died, leaving her estate to the father. The father died five months later. The son was executor for both estates. The estate tax return filed for the mother's estate reported that her estate passed to the father; the father's estate tax return included assets from the mother's estate. Later, the son petitioned the probate court for permission to disclaim on behalf of the father's estate and to reopen the mother's estate to receive the disclaimed assets. The probate court granted permission, but the disclaimer was ineffective for federal estate tax purposes.

Other cases involving an acceptance of benefits include

- Paying a beneficiary's personal bills using estate funds before that beneficiary's disclaimer of an interest in the estate.[96]
- Becoming general partner of a partnership before disclaiming the decedent's interest in that partnership (the disclaimant should have arranged to become the general partner in an arm's-length transaction after the decedent's interest had passed to the disclaimant's children).[97]

---

95. 726 F.2d 643 (10th Cir. 1984).

96. TAM 8405003. If the beneficiary had made only a partial disclaimer, it may have been qualified. PLR 9012053 (Where widow withdrew funds from a joint account, even though she subsequently repaid them, she accepted those funds, and she was foreclosed from disclaiming that half of the withdrawn amount and the income attributable to half of the amount withdrawn).

97. TAM 9123003.

- The exercise of a power of appointment was an acceptance of the trust property subject to the power, disqualifying a subsequent disclaimer of the trust property.[98]
- A beneficiary's direction to an executor to sell farmland that was part of the estate amounted to acceptance of the farmland, precluding a disclaimer of the sale proceeds, even though the executor could have ignored the direction.[99]
- Pledging an interest in an estate asset amounts to acceptance of that asset, precluding a later disclaimer of it, even if it was a short-term loan that was paid off before the distribution of the estate.[100]
- Becoming a general partner of a partnership is an acceptance of an interest in the partnership, precluding a qualified disclaimer.[101]
- Where a sister of a deceased insured who had named her as the beneficiary of his life insurance disclaimed 50 percent of the insurance proceeds so that 50 percent would pass by intestacy to the insured's daughter, acceptance lay in the fact that the estate's attorney had prepared the insurance application form, which the sister then signed, and the insurance company held the proceeds in an account on which it issued checks to the sister.[102]
- The quitclaim of a life estate in favor of only one remainderman constitutes acceptance.[103]
- The exercise of a power of appointment to any extent by the donee of the power is an acceptance of its benefits.[104] On the other hand, if the holder of a testamentary general power of appointment executes a will in which he provides for the exercise of the power, but just before the end of the nine-month period from the taxable transfer, he dis-

98. Est. of Engelman v. Comr., 121 T.C. 54 (2003).
99. Regs. § 25.2518-2(d)(4), Ex. 4.
100. Regs. § 25.2518-2(d)(4), Ex. 5.
101. TAM 9123003.
102. PLR 8702024.
103. TAM 8106013.
104. Regs. § 25.2518-2(d)(1).

claims the testamentary power, the exercise by will is not an acceptance because it is not effective until his death.[105]

- The reduction of a general power of appointment to a more limited power constitutes acceptance.[106]

Examples of consideration cases, which involve receiving different property in exchange for the disclaimer rather than somehow "touching" the disclaimed property itself, include the following:

- The acceptance of the actuarial present value by a disclaimant for her 2 percent income interest, which was to last until her death or remarriage, in the decedent's farmlands was consideration that disqualified her disclaimer of the 2 percent interest.[107]
- A beneficiary's disclaimer of her $4,000 income interest in a charitable trust (the presence of which disqualified the trust for the estate tax charitable deduction), in exchange for a lump sum equal to the cost of a $4,000 lifetime annuity, was not qualified.[108]
- Where a will devised certain real property to B and stated that any disclaimed property was to pass to C and B, and C agreed that B would disclaim all interest in the real property devised to him; and, in exchange, C promised to let B live in the family home for life, B's disclaimer was not a qualified disclaimer.[109]

---

105. Regs. § 25.2518-2(d)(4), Ex. 7. *See* TAM 8142008, which is consistent with this theory (executor cannot disclaim power exercised by decedent's will).

106. *See* Regs. §§ 25.2518-2(d)(1), 25.2518-3(a)(1)(iii), 25.2518-3(b), 25.2518-2(e)(1), and Goudy v. U.S., 86-2 USTC Para. 13,690 (D. Ore. 1986), *rev'd in unpub. opin.* (9th Cir. 6/28/88). *But see* Kunze Est. v. U.S., Docket No. 85-4173, D. Kan. (7/11/88).

107. Thompson Est. v. Comr., 89 T.C. 619 (1987), *rev'd on other grounds*, 864 F.2d 1128 (4th Cir. 1989). Since the disclaimant was not a qualified heir under special use valuation § 2032A, and her disclaimer was not qualified, the estate could not elect special use valuation for the farmlands, even though the consideration was paid by the decedent's daughters and not the estate.

108. PLR 7809043.

109. Regs. § 25.2518-2(d)(4), Ex. 2.

4. The Passage Test

There are two parts to the passage test. First, as a result of the disclaimer, the disclaimed interest must pass without any direction by the disclaimant.[110] Second, the disclaimed interest must pass to a person other than the disclaimant or to the transferor's spouse.[111] This second prong results in a double standard, in favor of the transferor's spouse, because he or she is the only one who can disclaim and still receive the disclaimed property in some form. For example, if a surviving spouse disclaims an outright gift under the deceased spouse's will, which provides that any property disclaimed by the surviving spouse passes to a trust for her benefit, the disclaimer will be qualified. The spouse cannot, however, have the power to direct where the trust property passes. Therefore, if, as a result of a spouse's disclaimer, the disclaimed property passes to a trust for her benefit over which she has a power of appointment, the disclaimer will not be qualified unless the spouse also disclaims the power of appointment.

A. No Direction

If there is an express or implied agreement that the disclaimed interest in property is to be given to a person specified by the disclaimant, the disclaimant will be treated as directing the transfer, and the disclaimer will not be qualified. On the other hand, precatory language in a disclaimer naming takers of the disclaimed property will not be considered as directing the redistribution or transfer of the property to the named takers if the applicable state law gives the language no legal effect.[112] For instance, assume a wife dies intestate, survived by her husband, daughter, and son. The husband disclaims his intestate share. His disclaimer includes language stating that it is his intention that the daughter and son will share equally in the disclaimed shares as a result of the disclaimer. If the state of the wife's residence considers these to be precatory words and gives them no legal effect, the husband is not

110. § 2518(b)(4); Regs. § 25.2518-2(e)(1).
111. § 2518(b)(4)(B), unless the disclaimant is the spouse of the decedent. § 2518(b)(4)(A).
112. Regs. § 25.2518-2(e)(4).

treated as directing the redistribution or transfer of the property. His disclaimer will not be disqualified because of his expression of his intention.[113]

A disclaimant can hold the power to distribute disclaimed property in a fiduciary capacity, if the power is limited by an ascertainable standard.[114] For instance, A creates an irrevocable trust naming B and C income beneficiaries for life and D as remainderman. D, as trustee, has the discretionary power to invade principal for the benefit of B and C. If D disclaims his remainder interest but retains his discretionary power of invasion, D has not made a qualified disclaimer. But if D may invade corpus only to make distributions for the health, maintenance, or support of B or C, then D's retained fiduciary power is limited by an ascertainable standard. D's disclaimer of his remainder interest, therefore, can be a qualified disclaimer.[115]

On the other hand, in a 1976 revenue ruling, a testator left the residue of his estate to his issue, with any disclaimed portion of the estate to be appointed by the disclaimant among the testator's issue and their spouses. The testator's son disclaimed his interest and appointed one-fourth to his deceased child's spouse and three-fourths to his deceased child's children. Because he directed where the disclaimed assets would pass, the son made a taxable transfer, not a qualified disclaimer.[116]

This problem can be fixed by disclaiming the right to appoint as well as the property interest itself. For example, a decedent who during his life had given 1,000 acres of his ranch to a charitable trust left the balance of his ranch to his children at his death. He also provided that if his children disclaimed any property of his

113. Regs. § 25.2518–2(e)(5), Ex. 8. *See* TAM 9509003 (precatory language naming taker of disclaimed property will not cause disclaimer to be disqualified; Illinois law applied); DePaoli v. Comr., 62 F.3d 1259 (10th Cir. 1995) (direction that disclaimed property pass to decedent's wife is precatory when property would pass to wife by intestacy; court determined that the disclaimant's illegitimate children were not the intestate heirs).

114. *Id.*

115. Regs. §§ 25.2518-2(e)(5), Exs. 11 and 12, 25.2518-3(d), Ex. 9.

116. Rev. Rul. 76-156, 1976-1 C.B. 292.

estate, that disclaimed property passed either to the charitable trust or to such other charitable organizations the children or the executor selected. The children disclaimed their interest in the ranch (except for the decedent's residence) and also disclaimed their right to select another charitable organization. In addition, the one child who was a coexecutor disclaimed her power as coexecutor to name another charity. The disclaimers were qualified.[117] This "double disclaimer" is also a useful technique for disclaimers in favor of a charity over which the disclaimant has the power to direct investments or distributions.[118]

Interests cannot be divided under the testamentary or other transfer document in a manner that allows the disclaimant to choose who will receive the disclaimed property. For example, if a will gives D the residuary estate in thirds and directs that a disclaimer of the first third passes to E, a disclaimer of the second passes to F, and a disclaimer of the third passes to G, then a disclaimer by D identifying which third of the residue he is disclaiming is a direction and therefore not qualified.[119]

However, a decedent can devise both Blackacre and Whiteacre to D and direct that if Blackacre is disclaimed, it passes to E; and if Whiteacre is disclaimed, it passes to F. D can make a qualified disclaimer of an undivided portion of both Blackacre and Whiteacre. More important, if D disclaims Blackacre with the intention that it pass to E, D's disclaimer can also be a qualified disclaimer.[120]

A disclaimer may not be effective to pass an interest in property to a person other than the disclaimant because the disclaimant also has the right to receive the property, or a portion of it, as

117. PLR 8624066.

118. *See, e.g.*, PLR 9008011 (Son disclaimed residuary estate under parent's will which passes, therefore, under parent's will to charitable foundation established by parent's will. Son's disclaimer will be qualified if he does not serve as co-trustee of the foundation; his wife and adult children can serve as co-trustees of the foundation.); and PLR 9532027 (disclaimer of property into donor-directed charitable fund will not pass at direction of disclaimant, since disclaimant only has the right to recommend the recipients of grants from the fund; the final decision is made by the charity).

119. Regs. § 25.2518-2(e)(5), Ex. 9.

120. Regs. § 25.2518-2(e)(5), Ex. 10.

the residuary beneficiary or intestate taker or by other means. In that event, the disclaimer is not qualified with respect to the portion of the disclaimed property that the disclaimant has a right to receive after the disclaimer.[121] A brother may disclaim his interest in bank accounts held in joint name of his father and himself. The bank account funds may pass, therefore, to the brother and sister, the only two heirs of the father who has died intestate or with a will that disposes of his estate in equal shares to his two children. The brother has made a qualified disclaimer of only 50 percent of the joint bank accounts.[122]

Further, if a father devises Blackacre to his son and provides a residuary trust, with income to his wife, remainder to the son; and the son disclaims Blackacre, which therefore becomes part of the residuary trust, the regulations state that the son's disclaimer will not be qualified unless he also disclaims "the remainder interest in the property."[123]

B. Horizontal and Vertical Slices

Disclaiming one portion of property while retaining another can cause the disclaimer not to be qualified. The regulations provide that, if the portion of the disclaimed interest in property that the disclaimant has a right to receive is not severable property or an undivided portion of the property, then the disclaimer is not qualified.[124] "Severable" property is that which can be divided into separate parts that, after the division, retain an independent

121. Regs. § 25.2518-2(e)(3). However, even if the non-spouse donee disclaims an inter vivos gift made shortly before the death of the donor, with the result that the gift falls into the donor's testamentary trust in which the non-spouse donee has an income or principal interest, the donee's disclaimer is qualified. Since the disclaimer would have been qualified if the donor had not died, the fact of the intervening death of the donor will not disqualify the disclaimer. PLR 9043050. *See also* PLR 200006052 (qualified disclaimers by all beneficiaries—including surviving spouse who, under decedent's will, would receive one-half of decedent's estate without contingencies but would forfeit the other half if she remarried—provide spouse, through intestate succession, with noncontingent interest in decedent's entire estate).

122. *See* Regs. § 25.2518-2(e)(5), Ex. 1.

123. Regs. § 25.2518-2(e)(3).

124. *Id.*

existence (for example, shares of stock: a block of 100 shares can be severed into two blocks of 50).[125] An "undivided" interest, on the other hand, must consist of a fraction or percentage of every substantial interest or right owned by the disclaimant and must extend over the entire period of the disclaimant's interest.[126]

The notion of severable property is straightforward. However, that of undivided property has caused some confusion. At least one court has distinguished between "horizontal" and "vertical slices" of property. A disclaimer of a vertical slice of pie—one that extends from the meringue to the crust—can be qualified, while the disclaimer of a horizontal slice (of the meringue only, for instance, that does not touch the crust) cannot be qualified.[127]

For instance, in the *Christiansen* case,[128] a decedent's will provided that her entire estate was to pass to her daughter, but that any property disclaimed by the daughter was to pass in part to a charitable lead trust and the balance outright to charity. The charitable trust lasted for twenty years, with the remainder interest passing to daughter. Daughter made a formula disclaimer of her outright gift, so that the disclaimed property passed to the charity and the charitable trust. However, she did not disclaim her remainder interest in the trust. Therefore, the disclaimer of the portion of property passing to the charitable trust was not qualified, while the disclaimer of the portion passing outright to the charity was. Note that the problem here may have been in the drafting: the decedent's plan stated that, following a disclaimer by the daughter, a charitable trust was created of which the daughter was a remainder beneficiary. The only way the disclaimer would have been qualified would have been for the daughter to have disclaimed her remainder interest in the trust as well.

For a further discussion of this issue, see section A of Chapter 6, addressing disclaimers of less than an entire interest.

---

125. Regs. § 25.2518-3(a)(1)(ii).
126. Regs. § 25.2518-3(b).
127. Walshire v. U.S., 288 F.3d 342, 347 (8th Cir. 2002).
128. Christiansen v. Comr., 130 T.C. 1 (2008).

C. Surviving Spouse as Disclaimant

Although the "no-interest" prong of the rule does not apply to a spouse who disclaims a transfer from a spouse, the "nondirection" prong does apply. The surviving spouse can disclaim an outright bequest under the deceased spouse's will even though the disclaimed bequest falls into a residuary trust that benefits the surviving spouse. However, as previously discussed, because the disclaimed interest must pass without any direction by the disclaimant, the spouse cannot have certain interests or powers with respect to that trust, including a lifetime or testamentary power of appointment.[129]

However, if the spouse is the trustee, the spouse can have discretionary powers as trustee to benefit both him or her and others if the powers are governed by an ascertainable standard.[130] The spouse can be the income beneficiary and can have power to invade trust principal for himself or herself[131] (bearing in mind that if the trust property is to be kept out of the spouse's estate, his power should be limited by an ascertainable standard[132]). The spouse can also disclaim in favor of a trust for his own benefit, over which the trustee (other than the spouse) has the power to distribute principal to the spouse, whether or not that power is limited by an ascertainable standard.[133]

If the spouse disclaims in favor of a trust that gives the spouse a lifetime or testamentary power, not limited by an ascertainable standard, "to direct the beneficial enjoyment of the disclaimed property in a transfer that is not subject to Federal estate and gift tax (whether as trustee or otherwise),"[134] the spouse must disclaim those powers over the disclaimed property passing to the trust. This portion must be determined by a fraction, the numerator of which is the fair market value of the disclaimed property on the

129. Regs. § 25.2518-2(e)(2).
130. Regs. § 25.2518-2(e)(5), Ex. 5.
131. Regs. § 25.2518-2(e)(2), (5), Ex. 6. This power is a general power of appointment. §§ 2041(a)(2), (b)(1), 2514(b), (c).
132. §§ 2041(b)(2), 2514(e).
133. Regs. § 25.2518-2(e)(5), Ex. 6.
134. Regs. § 25.2518-2(e)(2), (5), Exs. 5 and 7.

date of the disclaimer and the denominator of which is the total fair market value of the trust immediately after the disclaimer.[135]

In PLR 9440027, the IRS approved a partial disclaimer by the surviving spouse of a portion of the statutory share she received pursuant to an election against the decedent's will under New York law (which recognizes a partial exercise of the surviving spouse's right of election). The surviving spouse partially exercised the right to elect to take her share of the decedent's residuary estate and simultaneously renounced the right to elect a share of the decedent's transfer of any other dispositions in favor of others. In addition, the surviving spouse renounced the right to elect against every testamentary substitute or disposition other than the estate residue.

Finally, a disclaimer will not change the results of a general tax apportionment clause. In TAM 9502007, a spouse's disclaimer of specific assets did not change the character of those assets from part of the residuary estate into a specific bequest for purposes of the will's tax apportionment clause, since the decedent's will did not make a specific bequest of the disclaimed property or specify which assets were to go to a trust if there was a disclaimer, but merely provided where the residue would go if disclaimed. To avoid unintended estate tax results, the testator's will should address how the tax burden will fall on disclaimed property.

5. State Law Validity Test

Interestingly, state law validity of a disclaimer may not always be a requirement. For disclaimers that fail under local law, Section 2518(c)(3) permits a "written transfer," that otherwise meets the requirements for a qualified disclaimer, "of the transferor's entire interest in the property. . . to a person or persons who would have received the property had the transferor made a qualified disclaimer" to be treated as a qualified disclaimer. The final regulations also state that a disclaimer may be qualified even though not effective under local law,[136] but they also emphasize that under

135. Regs. § 25.2518-2(e)(5), Ex. 5.
136. Regs. § 25.2518-1(c)(1)(i).

applicable local law, the disclaimed interest in property be transferred, as a result of attempting the disclaimer, to another person without any direction on the part of the disclaimant. The regulations give an example of a disclaimer that is ineffective under local law, but that is still a qualified disclaimer. The local disclaimer statute provides that an untimely disclaimer is treated as an assignment of the interest disclaimed to those persons who would have taken the disclaimed interest had the disclaimer been valid. Absent that statutory provision, a would-be disclaimant's assignment to the same persons would not be a qualified disclaimer.[137]

Nevertheless, state requirements must be taken seriously (a local requirement that disclaimers must be filed in court, or state's "writing" requirements, for instance). If an executor, guardian, or conservator does not have the authority under state law to disclaim the estate's or ward's interest, the fiduciary certainly cannot transfer the interest.[138] The most significant state law issue is determining the identity of the taker of the disclaimed interest. Absent direction in the will or trust or other instrument of transfer creating the interest as to the disposition of the interest in the event of disclaimer, local law must be looked at to ascertain the identity of the taker in event of disclaimer.

137. Regs. § 25.2518-1(c)(3), Ex. 1.
138. *See* Rev. Rul. 90-110, 1990-2 C.B. 209.

6 SECTION 2518—SPECIFIC ISSUES

Aside from the complexity inherent in the general rules of disclaimer under Section 2518, additional complications arise when particular issues, such as disclaimers of smaller interests, are contemplated.

A. Disclaimers of Less than an Entire Interest: Undivided Portion, Separate Interest, and Severable Property

In general, Section 2518(c)(1) permits a disclaimer of an undivided portion of an interest. The regulations state that if the requirements of this section are met, the disclaimer of all or an undivided portion of any separate interest in property may be a qualified disclaimer even if the disclaimant has another interest in the same property. Each interest in property that is separately created by the transferor is treated as a separate interest.[1]

1. DISCLAIMING SOME TRUST INTERESTS BUT NOT OTHERS

Income and remainder interests in the same trust are separate interests unless, under local law, they merge.[2] What follows are some examples of disclaiming one interest while retaining another:

- A testamentary trust may provide that all of the income is paid, in such shares as the trustee may determine, to A and B, with all of the income payable at death of either to the other, and that the remainder be paid, at A's death, to B. B can disclaim his income interest and retain his remainder interest.[3]
- A power, including a power of appointment, is also a separate interest in property,[4] which also can be separately disclaimed.[5]

---

1. Regs. § 25.2518-3(a)(1)(i).

2. *Id.* For examples of merger, *see* Regs. § 25.2518-3(d), Ex. 12, and *compare* Exs. 13 and 14.

3. Regs. § 25.2518-3(d), Ex. 8. The purpose of this disclaimer may be to clean up the trust so that it will qualify as a qualified terminable interest property (QTIP) trust. *See also* PLR 200030012 (beneficiaries disclaim respective shares in discretionary distributions from deceased mother's testamentary trust during their father's lifetime, thus allowing the division of the trust into two separate shares, one qualifying as QTIP).

4. § 2518(c)(2); Regs. § 25.2518-3(a)(1)(iii). *See* PLR 200003023 (surviving spouse's power to withdraw or appoint revocable trust's assets, and her power to amend or revoke trust as to decedent's one-half interest in trust—decedent retained right to withdraw his one-half interest without accounting to spouse—constitute a lifetime power of appointment that is treated as a separate interest).

5. Regs. § 25.2518-3(d), Ex. 21. In TAM 9610005, the noncharitable beneficiary of a charitable remainder unitrust could disclaim his right to receive discretionary payments of principal, while retaining a right to unitrust payments that could include payments of principal. The disclaimer facilitated the reformation of the trust.

- If a person is both a permissible distributee of trust principal and a remainder beneficiary, she can disclaim her right to receive discretionary principal distributions but retain her remainder interest.[6]

However, the disclaimer of an interest, including a power, in property while retaining another power to direct the disposition of that property will not be a qualified disclaimer.[7] For instance, if H, who is the income beneficiary and the trustee of a trust, holds both the power to invade corpus for his health, maintenance, support, and happiness and a testamentary power of appointment, his disclaimer of the power of invasion, while retaining the testamentary power, is not a qualified disclaimer.[8] However, if H disclaimed the testamentary power and the retained power of invasion were limited by an ascertainable standard, H's disclaimer would be a qualified disclaimer.[9]

A disclaimant can disclaim his income interest in a trust of which he is the income beneficiary for life, or a percentage or fraction of his income interest,[10] or the first $5,000 of annual income from the trust, or all of the income in excess of the first $8,000 of annual income; but he cannot make a qualified disclaimer of his income interest for a term of years.[11]

The beneficiary of a trust cannot disclaim his income or principal interest in a specific asset held in the trust unless, as a result of the disclaimer and without any direction on the part of the disclaimant, the asset is removed from the trust.[12] In PLR 199944038, the IRS approved a disclaimer of interests in a trust where the disclaimed amounts passed to a charitable foundation (and trust beneficiaries who served on the foundation's board had no authority over the use of the funds).

6. Regs. § 25.2518-3(d), Ex. 11.
7. § 2518(b)(4); Regs. § 25.2518-2(e)(1).
8. Regs. § 25.2518-3(d), Ex. 9. *See also* Ex. 10.
9. Regs. § 25.2518-3(a)(1)(iii).
10. Regs. § 25.2518-3(d), Ex. 4.
11. Regs. § 25.2518-3(a)(1)(i).
12. Regs. § 25.2518-3(a)(2), (d), Exs. 5, 6, and 7.

2. Severable Property

A disclaimant can make a qualified disclaimer of a separate interest in property if the property is severable.[13] Severable property is property that can be divided into separate parts, each of which, after severance, maintains an independent existence. Examples are specific bequests to a named beneficiary of $50,000; household effects consisting of home furnishings, paintings, and silverware; 500 shares of stock in Z corporation; and a 500-acre farm. A beneficiary can make a qualified disclaimer, for instance, of $10,000; two of the paintings; 100 shares of Z corporation stock; and 300 identified acres or a fractional share of the farm.[14]

3. Partial Interests

A disclaimant may disclaim an undivided portion of a separate interest in property. The undivided portion must consist of a fraction or percentage of each and every substantial interest, or right owned by the disclaimant, in the separate interest in property and must extend over the entire term of the disclaimant's interest.[15]

The legatee of the residuary estate can disclaim specific assets that are part of the residuary estate, or a dollar share of the residuary estate or a percentage or fractional share.[16] The beneficiary of an outright gift of real property or securities cannot carve out an income interest and disclaim the remainder interest.[17] Therefore, the regulations also specify that if a partial disclaimer, either of a pecuniary amount or fractional share, is made of an interest in

---

13. Regs. § 25.2518-3(a)(1)(ii).
14. Regs. § 25.2518-3(d), Ex. 1.
15. Regs. § 25.2518-3(b). *See* PLR 9319022 for an example of a disclaimer of a portion of a bequest of stock under a formula.
16. Regs. § 25.2518-3(d), Exs. 1, 3, 17, and 19. *See also* PLR 199944038 (valid disclaimer where amount disclaimed is based on the value of a trust on the date of distribution, equal to a fraction of the trust interest disclaimed), and PLRs 199945010 and 199945012 (valid disclaimer of a fraction of the residuary estate that would have passed to a trust).
17. Regs. § 25.2518-3(b), (d), Ex. 2. *See, e.g.*, Walshire Est. v. U.S., 288 F.3d 342 (8th Cir. 2002) (taxpayer could not validly disclaim the remainder interest in his share of his brother's estate while reserving to himself the income and use of the property).

trust principal or other fund, the disclaimed portion must be segregated to ensure that no income attributable to the disclaimed portion reaches the disclaimant.[18]

The following partial disclaimers have been permitted by private letter rulings:

- The disclaimer by a wife of $120,000 of $418,632 in joint bank accounts on the death of her husband;[19]
- The disclaimer of a bequest of stock in a closely held corporation of the number of shares that qualify for redemption under Section 303 to pay taxes and expenses;[20] and
- The disclaimer by a son of all of his interest in his mother's residuary estate in excess of the amount necessary to repay his debt of $630,000.[21]

What is not permissible because there is no "separate interest . . . separately created by the transferor" is, for example, the disclaimer of a remainder interest in property received outright, with retention of a carved-out life estate;[22] or the disclaimer by a trust beneficiary of specific assets in a trust that continue to be held in trust.[23]

---

18. Regs. § 25.2518-3(c), (d), Exs. 17, 18, and 19. In PLR 199903019, the IRS approved a disclaimer of $2 million out of a bequest of $10 million. The disclaimed amount passed to a charitable trust controlled by the disclaimant. The money was segregated in a separate fund; the disclaimant had no control over the distribution of the funds and no authority over the members of the committee who disbursed the funds.
19. PLR 8208069.
20. PLR 8149050.
21. PLR 8113061.
22. Regs. § 25.2518-3(b), (d), Ex. 2. In *Walshire Est. v. U.S.*, 288 F.3d 342 (8th Cir. 2002), the Eighth Circuit upheld the validity of Regs. § 25.2518-3(b). A taxpayer had disclaimed the remainder interest in his share of his brother's estate while retaining an income interest in the disclaimed property. The taxpayer's estate conceded that the regulation precluded the decedent's disclaimer but argued that the regulation was inconsistent with § 2518(c), which permits a qualified disclaimer of an "undivided portion." The court held that a remainder interest is not an undivided portion and, thus, the regulation's prohibition of "horizontal" divisions was a reasonable construction of the statute.
23. Regs. § 25.2518-3(c), (d), Exs. 17, 18, and 19.

Some partial interests in trusts also can be disclaimed. In PLR 200840023, several children of a decedent, as conservators of minor grandchildren, disclaimed fractional interests in those trusts. As a result, the disclaimed property passed to the surviving spouse under a residuary clause. The Internal Revenue Service (IRS) ruled that the disclaimers were qualified and that, as a result, the property passing to the surviving spouse was treated as a transfer directly from the deceased spouse, qualifying for the estate tax marital deduction. Similarly, in a series of private rulings,[24] a daughter proposed to disclaim specific assets that otherwise would have passed to a trust for the daughter's benefit according to a decedent's exercise of a power of appointment. The exercise of the power stated that any property disclaimed by the daughter was to pass instead to a private foundation. Daughter proposed disclaiming specific assets that would pass to the trust for her benefit. The IRS ruled that, based on taxpayer representations, the disclaimer was qualified and that, because the daughter would have no power to direct the use of the disclaimed assets once they passed to the foundation, the gift of the disclaimed property passing to the foundation qualified for the estate tax charitable deduction in the decedent's estate.

4. Jointly Owned Property

In PLR 200618033, the disclaimant's husband died, survived by the disclaimant and two children (stepchildren of the disclaimant). The husband owned at his death rental real property, certificates of deposit (CDs), and four financial accounts that were titled in the husband's and disclaimant's names as joint tenants with rights of survivorship. The disclaimant stated that she did not contribute to the property, the CDs, or the four accounts and that, following the husband's death, she received no benefits from any of those assets. The husband's will provided that, if the disclaimant predeceased him, the residue of his estate would pass to the stepchildren. Within nine months of the husband's death, the disclaimant filed a disclaimer with the local court, disclaiming any interest in

24. *See, e.g.*, PLRs 201032002 and 201032010.

the real property, the CDs, and the husband's one-half interest in the joint accounts. The disclaimer emphasized that the disclaimant did not contribute to any of the joint accounts, and did not accept any benefit from the property after the husband's death, including any income generated by those assets after that time.

Even in the case of titling changes and accepting of certain benefits, disclaimers can be made. In PLR 200503024, husband and wife created a brokerage account as joint tenants with rights of survivorship. The account held publicly traded securities. One month after husband's death, wife's broker told her that the joint account could no longer be held in the deceased husband's social security number, and wife instructed the broker to change title into the wife's name alone. Over the next seven months, the wife directed the broker to buy and sell certain securities, and she took out cash. In the ninth month after the husband's death, the wife, after consulting with her lawyer, disclaimed her beneficial survivorship interest in the brokerage account, but reduced by the assets in that share (including the post-death earnings on those assets) from which wife accepted benefits. The disclaimer was recorded and delivered to the broker.

Following the disclaimer, the broker was instructed to create three accounts: (1) a "TIC" account (held as tenants in common between wife and husband's estate, and consisting of assets that could not be evenly divided, and did not include any assets bought or sold after husband's death); (2) wife's account (that included both wife's half of the assets, plus those assets attributable to husband that wife had directed to be bought or sold after husband's death); and (3) the estate account (that consisted of assets attributable to husband with respect to which wife made no withdrawals and did not direct any sales). Following the disclaimer, the estate's one-half interest in the tenancy in common (TIC) account and the estate account were used to fund the credit shelter trust. Wife was a co-trustee of that trust with husband's children, and she could never serve as sole trustee.

Because wife followed the right steps, the IRS approved the disclaimer. First, merely changing the title into the wife's name did not constitute acceptance. Second, the cash and securities were severable assets, so the wife could accept the benefits of cash withdrawals and still disclaim other assets. Third, although the wife is deemed to have accepted benefits over securities she directed the broker to buy, she could still disclaim the one-half interest in the securities that remained after her husband's death because the securities were severable. Finally, although the wife was a trustee, and a trustee could make discretionary distributions, she could never exercise that power solely, so serving in that role did not disqualify the disclaimer.

The key to this successful disclaimer was segregating the assets; the IRS obviously would not have approved the disclaimer if the assets over which the wife exercised control were a part of it.

5. Disclaiming Powers of Appointment

In PLR 200825037, a trust created before October 22, 1942, was created for the benefit of the daughter and gave her a general power of appointment over the trust property. If she failed to exercise that power, the trust property passed into further trusts for the benefit of grandchildren. Those trusts would last for their lifetimes, and each grandchild had general powers of appointment over them. At each grandchild's death, his or her trust property passed into further trust for great-grandchildren. The taxpayers proposed that the daughter would allow her general power of appointment to lapse (which, because it was a general power created before October 22, 1942, would not result in the trust property being included in her estate)[25] and each grandchild would disclaim his or her general power of appointment, so that, at the daughter's death, each grandchild would have a trust for his or her benefit, but the trust property would not be included in his or her estate at death. The IRS approved.

This otherwise routine private ruling is interesting only because it serves as a reminder that, while the nine-month clock on disclaimers generally starts running on the date the original irrevocable document is created, it does not start running when it follows a general power of appointment until after the exercise, release, or lapse of that general power.

25. *See generally* §§ 2041 and 2514.

In PLR 200832018, the surviving spouse (wife) disclaimed assets in a joint brokerage account (other than those over which she exercised some measure of control before executing the disclaimer) so that they would pass instead into a shelter trust and marital trust under the husband's revocable trust. Wife also disclaimed her testamentary limited powers of appointment over both trusts, so that the disclaimers of the brokerage account assets would be qualified (that is, because the disclaimed property must pass "without direction" by the disclaimant in order for the disclaimer to be qualified, the disclaimant cannot hold a power to appoint property of a trust into which disclaimed property has passed). This ruling provides a good example of how to (1) disclaim assets in a joint account over which the disclaimant already has exercised some measure of control; and (2) use disclaimers to "prepare" the trust into which disclaimed property is to pass.

B. Fiduciary as Disclaimant

The already complicated disclaimer issues become even more convoluted when a fiduciary is involved. Fiduciaries can become involved with disclaimers by administering disclaimed property, by disclaiming trust property, or by disclaiming trust powers. Each has different complications, discussed below.

1. Disclaimant as Fiduciary of Disclaimed Interest

A disclaimant may also be a fiduciary of the disclaimed property. For instance, if a child disclaims property that then passes to a residuary trust of which she is the trustee and her children are beneficiaries, her fiduciary power to make discretionary distributions must be limited by an ascertainable standard.[26] Otherwise, the disclaimer is not qualified.[27] One way to cure the problem is for the disclaimant to refuse to serve as trustee, allowing another

26. *Compare* Exs. (11) and (12) of Regs. § 25.2518-2(e)(5).
27. § 2518(b)(4)(B); Regs. § 25.2518-2(e)(1).

family member to serve instead.[28] A disclaimant can, under some circumstances, remain as coexecutor of the estate without causing the disclaimer to be disqualified,[29] and a disclaimer in favor of a private foundation of which the disclaimant is a trustee is qualified if the disclaimant retains no discretionary power to affect enjoyment of the interest.[30]

2. Fiduciary as Beneficiary of Disclaimer

An executor may disclaim on behalf of her decedent's estate or as guardian or conservator on behalf of her minor or incompetent ward and, in doing so, may benefit herself. This presents no problem under the "no-interest rule" of Section 2518(b) because the disclaimer is done in a fiduciary, not an individual, capacity.

For instance, where a husband and wife died in rapid succession, the daughter, who was the sole beneficiary of the second estate and of the first estate if there were no surviving spouse, could, as executor of the second estate, make a qualified disclaimer of the interest of the surviving spouse in the estate of the first spouse to die.[31] A niece, who was the sole beneficiary of her aunt's estate and of her uncle's, if her aunt had not survived him, could, as executor of her aunt's estate, make a qualified disclaimer of a portion, with a value of approximately $1,500,000, of the uncle's estate on behalf of the aunt's estate. The ruling states that although niece will be the recipient of the disclaimed property, the disclaimer does not violate Section 2518(b)(4). Niece will act in her fiduciary capacity as the personal representative of aunt and aunt's estate. Thus, niece is disclaiming on behalf of aunt and aunt's estate and is receiving the property in her individual capacity as the beneficiary of uncle's estate.[32]

28. Rev. Rul. 76-156, 1976-1 C.B. 292.
29. PLR 9319022.
30. PLR 200149015.
31. PLR 9015017, PLR 7937011.
32. PLR 8749041.

3. Authority of Fiduciary to Disclaim

A fiduciary does not have a common law right to disclaim property she holds in a fiduciary capacity; that right has to be given either by the instrument transferring the interest to be disclaimed, by state statute or court order, by the durable power of attorney executed by the adult ward while competent, or by a decedent's distributees.[33] For example, a niece, who as executor of her aunt's estate planned to disclaim a portion of her uncle's estate in order to benefit herself, was authorized by the Oklahoma statute that permitted disclaimer by an "executor . . . of the estate of a . . . deceased beneficiary, if he deems it in the best interests of those interested in the estate of such beneficiary and of those who take the beneficiary's interest by virtue of the disclaimer . . . with or without an order of the probate court."[34]

4. Disclaiming of Fiduciary Power

When a trustee is disclaiming a fiduciary power, Rev. Rul. 90-110 provides that appropriate authorization must be obtained if the disclaimer is to be qualified.[35] Further, if the power to be disclaimed by the fiduciary is beneficial to a particular beneficiary, that beneficiary also must disclaim.[36] For instance, a bypass trust

---

33. Hoenig Est. v. Comr., 66 T.C. 471 (1976), *acq.*, 1978-1 C.B. 1 (State statute authorizing disclaimer by executors of husband's estate of husband's interest in estate of wife who had predeceased him by a few days was not required, since executors disclaimed with consent of the beneficiary of husband's will). *See* Cleaveland v. U.S., 88-1 USTC Para. 13,766 (C.D. Ill. 1988).

34. PLR 8749041. *See* PLR 8737034 (executor of estate of deceased trust beneficiary, whose death followed shortly upon the death of the testator whose will created the trust, "had authority under applicable law" to disclaim the beneficiary's general power of appointment granted to him by the trust).

35. 1990-2 C.B. 209 (Decedent's will provided a trust for surviving spouse that was not a QTIP trust, because the trustee was given the power to invade corpus for the benefit of a grandchild. Because grandchild did not consent to trustee's disclaimer nor make an individual disclaimer and decedent's will did not authorize trustee's disclaimer, trustee's disclaimer is ineffective under local law and is not a qualified disclaimer).

36. *Id.*, citing Bogert, The Law of Trusts and Trustees § 150 (Rev. 2d ed. 1979) and Restatement (Second) of Trusts § 102(4) (1959).

in a much older will may direct that all of the income be paid to the surviving spouse and may give the trustee the discretionary power to invade the corpus for the spouse and the decedent's children. The bypass trust does not qualify as a QTIP trust, because the trustee can distribute principal to the children during the spouse's lifetime. Disclaimers must be executed by the trustee and by the permissible objects (e.g., the children) of the power.[37] If the trustee is the sole beneficiary of the disclaimed power, then only the signature of the trustee is necessary for the disclaimer to be qualified. For example, in PLR 9521032, a surviving spouse wished to disclaim his right, as trustee of his spouse's trust, to distribute principal to himself. Such a disclaimer is qualified if the surviving spouse made the disclaimer both as trustee and beneficiary of the trust.

C. Failure to Assert Right as Disclaimer?

Some beneficiaries obtain rights automatically as a result of a decedent's death. The most common such right is the elective share for surviving spouses. This raises the question whether a surviving spouse must affirmatively disclaim his elective share right in order to avoid having made a taxable transfer by not having exercised it. A revenue ruling issued before the enactment of Section 2518 held that an executor's failure to assert his or her right to commissions was effective as an implied waiver for the executor's own gift and income tax purposes.[38] It is unclear whether the rationale still holds after the enactment of that statute. A similar question

37. *See, e.g.*, TAM 8729002; TAM 8605004; TAM 8549004; TAM 8527009. *Compare* Lassiter Est. v. Comr., T.C. Memo 2000-324 (Georgia law provisions enabling trusts to qualify for marital deduction and surviving spouse's disclaimer of inter vivos special power of appointment, together with disclaimers by other family members, allowed pre-ERTA (Economic Recovery Tax Act) trust to qualify for QTIP election; because Georgia law eliminated impermissible fiduciary powers held by the wife as trustee, court did not address validity of wife's disclaimer, as trustee, of certain fiduciary powers over trust).

38. Rev. Rul. 66-167, 1966–1 C.B. 20.

arises in regard to the failure to contest a will on plausible grounds of incompetency or undue influence. In neither case should a disclaimer be required, and two 1988 Louisiana decisions are helpful. In *Longue Vue Foundation v. Comr.*,[39] and *Harvey Est. v. U.S.*,[40] the IRS challenged the estates' charitable deductions on the ground that the decedents' heirs had not disclaimed their forced heirship, which, if claimed, would have reduced the amount of the charitable bequests. The taxpayer won in both cases. Neither case was appealed.

In TAM 8015015, a husband and wife had executed a joint and mutual will. After the husband's death, the wife modified her will to provide for a charitable bequest. On audit, the IRS estate tax attorney denied a charitable deduction for the wife's estate. He asserted that the wife was bound by the joint and mutual will, that heirs under the joint and mutual will could contest the modified will, and that they should have filed a timely disclaimer. The IRS, however, allowed the charitable deduction, stating that: "Section 2518 . . . is applicable only where there is, at a minimum, some claim or right or interest in the property by some individual." No such interest existed here because, until a beneficiarytook further action, nothing would pass to him. Thus, there can be no allegation that a beneficiary under the original joint and mutual will made a transfer subject to the gift tax for failure to file a disclaimer.

Rev. Rul. 74-492[41] also provides the right answer, but with some troubling language. Husband died in 1972 with a will that made no provision for the wife, who died two months later without having exercised her elective share rights. The IRS ruled that the wife neither possessed an interest in property within the meaning of Section 2033 nor a general power of appointment under Section 2041.[42] The ruling states that the failure to assert the inchoate right constitutes a complete and effective disclaimer or renunciation of a power of appointment by operation of law.[43] This is

39. 90 T.C. 150 (1988), *acq. in result only*, 1989-1 C.B. 1.
40. 678 F. Supp. 1268 (1988).
41. 1974-2 C.B. 298.
42. *Id.* at 299.
43. *Id.*

troubling because, if the failure to assert an inchoate right was a disclaimer by operation of law in 1972, now that the federal tax law of disclaimer has been codified in Section 2518, the procedural requirements of Section 2518 arguably apply.

TAM 8442006 is an unfavorable ruling in which a decedent had died in 1980, survived by two adult children and the children of a predeceased child who, under Louisiana law, were "forced heirs." The decedent's will left 87 percent of her estate to charity and the balance to the children and grandchildren, which was less than the full amount of their forced share. The IRS denied the charitable deduction to the extent of the estate that could have been, but wasn't, claimed by the forced heirs.

The IRS cited in support of its holding *Bel v. U.S.*, a Fifth Circuit case involving the amount of the marital deduction allowable to the estate of a Louisiana resident who died in 1961.[44] In *Bel*, the decedent's will gave to his wife one-half of his estate. Under Louisiana law, the decedent's children had forced heirship rights to two-thirds of his estate and the right to reduce the bequest to their mother. As Section 2056 was then written, property passing to the surviving spouse because of a disclaimer would be deemed to have passed from the disclaimant and not from the deceased spouse. The district court had found that the children disclaimed that portion of their legitime that was impinged upon by the bequest to their mother and, because of the then Section 2056, denied a marital deduction for the amount disclaimed.[45] The Fifth Circuit found no disclaimer, but instead a quid pro quo agreement in which the children agreed to renounce their legitime in exchange for the surrender by their mother of some interests.[46] The Fifth Circuit stated that "without more the very existence of the children's forced heirship rights would prohibit the taxpayers from claiming a marital deduction in an amount greater than the value of the decedent's

44. 452 F.2d 683 (5th Cir. 1971). The principal concern of the court was for an entirely different issue: whether the decedent's payment of the premium for an accidental death policy acquired by the decedent's children within one year of the decedent's death constituted a transfer by the decedent. 452 F.2d at 686.

45. 310 F. Supp. 1189 (W.D. La. 1970).

46. 452 F.2d at 693.

net disposable estate,"[47] citing, in support of this dictum, the terminable interest rule of Section 2056(b)(1)(A). Despite this Fifth Circuit opinion, on which the 1984 TAM had relied, the taxpayers who were the targets of this TAM challenged it in the tax court case of *Longue Vue Foundation v. Comr.*[48] and won.

Therefore, there may be more than one answer to the question asked at the beginning of this section. A qualified disclaimer should not be required if an affirmative right has not been asserted. If an heir with standing to contest a will does not do so, he should not be deemed to have made a transfer to those who take under the will because he did not disclaim that right. The facts of a 1987 private letter ruling may be read as in support of this proposition. The son proposed to disclaim a bequest under his father's will which therefore would pass to a discretionary trust for the benefit of the son's children. The ruling states that the son *will refuse to serve as trustee* of the discretionary trust, not that the son will disclaim his right to serve as trustee.[49]

---

47. *Id.*
48. 90 T.C. 150 (1988), *acq. in result only*, 1989-1 C.B. 1.
49. PLR 8736024.

7 GENERAL TRANSFER TAX USES OF DISCLAIMER

Now that the basics of Section 2518 have been discussed, this chapter reviews the ways in which this technique can be used to help in the estate planning and administration process.

A. Generally—Changing the Dispositive Plan

If a beneficiary of a gift wants to redirect that gift to another beneficiary, either because there was a drafting error and the initial beneficiary was not the intended beneficiary or because the initial beneficiary does not need the money, she faces a problem. If she accepts the gift and then gives that property to the next beneficiary, the initial beneficiary has made a taxable gift. To avoid this penalty on generosity, the beneficiary can disclaim the gift instead.

Many disclaimers are simply altruistic. For example, the stepmother of a pilot killed in Vietnam disclaimed so that the pilot's years of missing in action

(MIA) back pay passed to his descendants;[1] a brother disclaimed his one-half share of his father's intestate estate so that it could pass in part to his sister;[2] and so on.[3] Beyond those examples, there are more sophisticated reasons for disclaimers.

1. To Rewrite a Will or Rearrange Disposition of Non-Probate Assets

If a will contains an inappropriate gift, either by drafting error or changed circumstances, the heirs can disclaim that gift to essentially rewrite the will. In *Boyd Est. v. Comr.*,[4] the father executed a will that gave his estate to his wife, with his son as contingent beneficiary. The father's insurance policy named the same beneficiaries. After his wife's death, the father remarried but failed to rewrite his will and his insurance beneficiary designation. When the father died, the son disclaimed his gift under the will, including the benefit of the tax apportionment provision of the will which directed that death taxes on the insurance be paid from the residuary estate, in order to provide for his stepmother. The Internal Revenue Service (IRS) challenged the son's disclaimer with respect to the estate taxes on the insurance policy, arguing that the tax apportionment direction was not an interest in property within the meaning of Section 2518. However, the Seventh Circuit held that the son, who had backed up his disclaimer by giving the executor a check for the estimated tax due, had made a qualified disclaimer of this amount.

The following are other examples of disclaimers made to change or correct an estate plan:

- A disclaimer of the benefit conferred by a decedent's waiver of the Section 2207A right of recovery would be a

1. PLR 7909055.
2. PLR 8648070.
3. *See, e.g.*, PLR 8908022 and PLR 8824033.
4. 819 F.2d 170 (7th Cir. 1987), *rev'g* 85 T.C. 1056 (1985). *See also* Anderson Est. v. Comr., 56 T.C.M. 78 (1988) (to carry out deceased husband's wishes not expressed in his will, which gave everything to widow, widow and son agreed not to probate will and filed affidavit of heirship, backed up by widow's timely disclaimer of all of her interests under the will).

qualified disclaimer if the disclaimer otherwise met the Section 2518 requirements.[5]

- A testator left her estate equally to Y and Z, and also held a certificate of deposit in her name in trust for Y. Y disclaimed his interest in the certificate of deposit so that the funds would fall into the residuary estate and pass equally to Y and to Z.[6]
- A decedent left a gift of X Corporation stock to his son, a limited bequest for his wife, and the residue to his daughter. The son disclaimed some of the shares of stock, which became part of the residue, and his interest in the intestate estate. The daughter disclaimed her entire interest in the residue except for a smaller number of shares of the stock, and her intestate interest. As a result, the son and daughter ended up sharing the bequest of X Corporation stock and everything else passed to their mother.[7]
- A noncitizen son of a U.S. citizen can disclaim a bequest from the parent, so that it passes to the son's children who do not reside in the country in which the disclaimant resides and therefore are not subject to the same restrictive laws of that country.[8]
- A surviving spouse, two of the decedent's children, the decedent's eight grandchildren, and two of decedent's nieces all executed qualified disclaimers in order to include a pretermitted heir in a share of the decedent's estate.[9]
- A will gave the surviving spouse a general power of appointment over what was intended to be a credit shelter trust. The surviving spouse disclaimed the power to ensure that the trust assets were not included in her gross estate.[10]
- A testator's will created a trust that was intended to qualify for qualified terminable interest property (QTIP) treatment

5. PLR 200127007.
6. PLR 8525016. *See also* PLR 9043050, PLR 9044062, and PLR 8824033.
7. PLR 8510023.
8. Steiner, *Disclaimers: Post-Mortem Creativity*, 4 PROB. & PROP. 43, 44 (Nov–Dec. 1990).
9. PLR 200028020.
10. PLR 8603030.

but that gave the testator's daughter an invasion power.[11] The daughter's disclaimer of her right to receive property from the trust resulted in the trust qualifying for the marital deduction.[12]

2. Control of Family Business

Disclaimers can be used to pass ownership or control of a family business on to the next generation, or to affect rights under a shareholder's agreement. For instance, in PLR 8107073, a mother, who owned 50 percent of the stock of a family corporation, inherited the other 50 percent. She disclaimed her inherited 50 percent, which then passed to the son, and had her own 50 percent redeemed in a Section 302 complete termination of interest redemption.

B. Fixing the Marital Deduction

Disclaimers can fix some, but not all, trusts intended to qualify for QTIP treatment but that do not meet all of the Section 2056(b)(7) requirements.[13] For some reason, lawyers have drafted a lot of "pot" trusts that have as current beneficiaries both the surviving spouse and others (typically children and grandchildren). While there may be sound reasons for creating such trusts in certain circumstances,[14] in the marital context this generally is not a good idea because use of a pot trust obviously prevents the trust from

11. PLR 8337069.

12. *See* Bucquet v. Livingston, 57 Cal. App. 3d 914, 129 Cal. Rptr. 514 (1976) (lawyer was liable to decedent's beneficiaries for damages ensuing from (1) lawyer's malpractice in drafting testamentary bypass trust for surviving spouse with a general, rather than a special, power of appointment; and (2) as lawyer employed to probate decedent's will, in not advising surviving spouse to disclaim her power of appointment).

13. *See, e.g.*, PLRs 9003007, 9018046, and 9629023.

14. For example, the size of the husband's and wife's combined estates are not large enough to generate an estate tax, one of the beneficiaries has a physical disability that may require access to all trust funds, or the trust is a "dynasty" trust and is exempt from estate and generation-skipping transfer tax.

qualifying for the marital deduction under Section 2056. Alternatively, all trust beneficiaries may disclaim their trust interests so that the property passes outright to the spouse by intestacy. Children have disclaimed their right to receive discretionary or mandatory distributions of income or principal during the surviving spouse's life;[15] guardians for minor children have been permitted to disclaim, on behalf of their wards, a fractional portion of the children's rights as beneficiaries of trustees' discretionary powers;[16] and, where the decedent's family was given the right to support from the bypass trust for the decedent's wife, if members of the family executed qualified disclaimers of their interest, the trust would be eligible for QTIP election.[17]

Note, however, that not all disclaimer solutions are workable.[18] In TAM 9818005, for example, disclaimers failed to transform a residuary trust under a pre-ERTA (Economic Recovery Tax Act) will into a QTIP trust. The decedent's adult children and a guardian ad litem for his minor children and unborn descendants disclaimed the right to receive the income or principal of the residuary trust during the surviving spouse's lifetime. The spouse, who served as trustee, also disclaimed her lifetime power to appoint trust property and any right to have trust income withheld from her. However, although the spouse was the only permissible trust beneficiary during her life, the IRS ruled that she did not have a qualifying income interest for life under Section 2056(b)(7). The RESTATEMENT (SECOND) OF

15. TAM 9003007; PLR 8906036; PLR 8824066; PLR 8817031; PLR 8637044; TAM 8546007. *See* Cleaveland v. U.S., 88-1 USTC Para. 13,766 (C.D. Ill. 1988) (trustee's disclaimer of power to invade principal for benefit of children, in order to make residuary trust eligible for QTIP election, worked, although children (all adult) did not disclaim; children would be estopped to claim benefits under power because they knew of trustee's disclaimer and did not object). *See also* TAM 9247002 (children's disclaimers of discretionary income and principal distributions qualified trust for § 2056(b)(7) QTIP marital deduction); Lassiter Est. v. Comr., T.C. Memo 2000-324 (descendants' disclaimers of rights to income and principal during surviving spouse's lifetime, together with spouse's disclaimer of inter vivos special power of appointment and facilitating provisions of Georgia law, qualified pre-ERTA trust for QTIP election).

16. TAM 9003007; PLRs 8725063 and 8704023.

17. PLR 8704023.

18. *See, e.g.*, PLR 9818005.

TRUSTS provides that a trustee may not accept a trust in part and disclaim the rest of it, and Rev. Rul. 90-110[19] ruled that a trustee's attempt to disclaim the right to make distributions to a beneficiary was not effective unless it was permitted by local law or the governing instrument. Therefore, the decedent's will created no such disclaimer right in the trustee, and local law did not permit such disclaimers by fiduciaries. Because the spouse's disclaimer as trustee was ineffective under state law, it was not a qualified disclaimer, and the trustee could invest in unproductive property and apportion receipts between income and principal, in violation of Regs. § 20.2056(b)-5(f)(1) and -5(f)(4).

In another case,[20] the wife's will established an irrevocable trust designed to accept retirement benefits for the surviving spouse. This trust then terminated on the surviving spouse's death and was distributable to a second trust for the benefit of the decedent's children. Later, the wife executed beneficiary designations naming the children, not the first trust, as retirement plan beneficiaries. The children disclaimed their interests in the retirement plans, and because no contingent beneficiaries were named, the benefits passed to the first trust. However, the children failed to disclaim their interests in the second trust. As a result, they did not disclaim their entire interests in the retirement plan benefits, so the disclaimers were not qualified.

Occasionally a bypass trust must first be severed into two trusts or shares in order for one of them to qualify for the QTIP election. For example, in PLR 8815038, a husband's residuary trust provided that 50 percent of the income be payable to his wife, with principal payable if necessary to bring distributions to his wife up to $1,000 a month. The other 50 percent of trust income was payable equally to the two children or their issue. The trustee was given the power to invade principal for the wife and the two children. At the wife's death, the trust corpus was payable to the two children or their issue. The taxpayer proposed that the children would disclaim their right to benefit from the trustee's power of invasion of principal from one-half of the trust during the wife's

19. 1990-2 C.B. 209.
20. PLR 200846003.

lifetime. The trust would then be split into two trusts. Trust A would pay all of the income to the wife. Trust B would pay so much of the income to the wife as needed to bring her monthly distributions up to $1,000. The trustee would have the power to invade Trust A for the wife but for no one else. Income of Trust B, to the extent not needed to supplement Trust A income in order to bring the wife's monthly distributions up to $1,000, would be payable to the children, and the trustee could invade the principal of Trust B for the children. With all of this accomplished, Trust A would be eligible for the QTIP election.[21]

In addition to fixing trusts, disclaimers also can be used to create or increase outright spousal gifts that qualify for marital deduction treatment. For example, a decedent's children disclaimed their intestate interest, except for an amount sheltered by the unified credit, in order to increase their mother's intestate share and thereby reduce the tax on the decedent's estate to zero.[22] Children have, similarly, disclaimed interests under their father's will, in order to increase the amount passing to their mother under the

21. *See also* PLRs 199994023, 9018046, 9010062, and 8824066 (children will disclaim a fractional portion of their interests in decedent's "family trust" as discretionary beneficiaries of income and principal of trust (but not their interests as contingent remaindermen upon death of their mother), leaving mother as sole current beneficiary of the disclaimed portion; the disclaimed portion will be severed and administered separately and will be eligible for QTIP election).

22. *See, e.g.*, PLRs 8729008, 8514095, and 8409089. *Compare* TAM 8701001 (disclaimers of intestate interest by adult children and court-appointed guardian of minor children, with court permission, were effective to increase surviving spouse's share of deceased spouse's intestate estate and to increase the marital deduction) *with* TAM 8926001 (IRS rejected lower state court ruling that disclaimer of intestate interests by the three adult children resulted in increasing surviving spouse's intestate share, and ruled that the disclaimed intestate shares passed to the minor grandchildren), and Hunt v. U.S., 566 F. Supp. 356 (E.D. Ark. 1983).

residuary estate or by intestacy.[23] In TAM 9228004, an agreement between the surviving spouse and his sons not to probate the decedent's will, coupled with the sons' disclaimers of their remainder interests in a testamentary trust paying income to the spouse, resulted in the property passing to the surviving spouse as a result of the sons' disclaimers qualifying for the marital deduction. There are other more recent examples of other beneficiaries disclaiming their interests in trusts so that the surviving spouse is sole beneficiary[24] and of family members disclaiming outright gifts so that the property passes outright to the surviving spouse.[25]

1. Eligibility for Marital Deduction of Spouse's Interest in Charitable Remainder Trust

Section 2056(b)(8) is an exception to the terminable interest rule of Section 2056(b)(1): If a surviving spouse is given an annuity in a charitable remainder trust, the annuity qualifies for the marital deduction as long as the surviving spouse is the only noncharitable beneficiary of the trust,[26] or the only beneficiary of the trust who is not an employee stock ownership plan (ESOP) beneficiary (as defined in Section 2056(b)(8)(B)(ii)).[27]

---

23. *See, e.g.*, Maddox v. U.S., 81-1 USTC Para. 13,391 (N.D. Ohio 1981); Newman Est. v. Comr., 38 T.C.M. 898 (1979), *aff'd in unpub. opin.* (5th Cir. 1980), *cert. denied* (1981); Hankins Est. v. Comr., 42 T.C.M. 229 (1981). In each of these three cases, the attempted disclaimer, governed by pre–§ 2518 disclaimer law, failed because of failure to abide by requirements of the applicable state disclaimer law. *See also, e.g.*, PLRs 9051007, PLR 8831032, and PLR 8719014; TAMs 8714010, 8639002, and 8347001; PLR 8301040.

24. *See, e.g.*, PLRs 200505030 and 200604003.

25. *See, e.g.*, PLR 200626002.

26. § 2056(b)(8)(A).

27. § 2056(b)(8), as amended by Pub. L. No. 105–34, § 1530(c)(8), effective for transfers made by trusts to, or for the use of, an ESOP after August 5, 1997.

2. Ineligibility for the Marital Deduction of Gift to Noncitizen Spouse

Section 2056(d) denies the estate tax marital deduction for property passing to a noncitizen spouse unless that property passes to or is transferred into a qualified domestic trust (QDT) that meets the requirements of Section 2056A. Under Section 2056(d)(2), property passing to a noncitizen spouse can be transferred by him to a QDT that he created. Therefore, there is likely to be little use of a disclaimer in this situation.

However, the gift tax provisions with respect to noncitizen spouses are different. Section 2523(i) eliminates the gift tax marital deduction for gifts to noncitizen spouses, and Section 2515 treats transfers to a noncitizen spouse of a joint property interest or a tenancy by the entirety interest in real property as non-gifts until the termination, other than by death, of the joint interest. In addition, there is an annual exclusion for gifts to a noncitizen spouse, so a noncitizen spouse might want to disclaim the gift to reduce the gift to the amount of that exclusion.

C. Planning for the Tax Relief, Unemployment Reauthorization, and Job Creation Act of 2010

Many advisors (the author included) were certain that the one-year repeal of the federal estate and generation-skipping transfer taxes in 2010 would never happen, that Congress could not allow such a "train wreck" to occur.[28] Yet that is exactly what happened: Although the House passed a bill under which the law as it existed in 2009 would have continued on at least a temporary basis, the Senate did not address that bill. As a result, the two federal taxes really did go away for a year. In December 2010, Congress finally enacted legislation reinstating the federal estate

28. *See, e.g.*, Kaufman, *2010: The Anatomy of a Train Wreck*, 37 Estate Planning 42 (May 2010).

and generation-skipping transfer taxes as well as adding some other significant changes.[29] These changes, however, are in place only until December 31, 2012.

Before digging into some of the changes in 2010 tax act, the most important point to make is that Congress still has no cohesive, permanent structure in place for federal transfer taxes. Worse, tax advisors have dealt with uncertainty for so long (going back to the 2001 tax act, the Economic Growth and Tax Relief Reconciliation Act, or EGTTRA, that started it all) that, even if Congress were to create a permanent system for those taxes, many of those advisors would find it difficult to take it seriously. This lack of confidence makes flexible planning more important than ever. And this is where disclaimers can come in very handy.

With the cumbersome name of the Tax Relief, Unemployment Reauthorization, and Job Creation Act of 2010, (hereafter the "2010 Act"), there are some highlights to consider when planning with disclaimers. First and most important, the 2010 Act allows for a $5 million exemption from estate, gift, and generation-skipping transfer taxes. So, as an initial matter, the 2010 Act takes the vast majority of Americans out of the federal transfer tax system (at least until 2013). Second, the 2010 Act allows for the "portability" of exemption between spouses, allowing a surviving spouse to use both his or her exemption as well as that of the predeceased spouse, for a total of $10 million of exemption (assuming that neither spouse used any exemption for gift tax purposes during life). On its face, at least, this provision eliminates the need for a "credit shelter" trust to protect the predeceased spouse's exemption from estate taxes, at least for federal purposes.

There are many problems with the 2010 Act, most of which are beyond the scope of this discussion. However, even assuming that there were no other problems with the 2010 Act, for our purposes there are two important points to consider:

1. The 2010 Act provisions don't apply after 2012; and
2. The 2010 Act does nothing for protection against state inheritance or estate tax.

---

29. *See, e.g.*, Kaufman, *Finally, Legislation! Congress Kicks the Can Down the Road*, 38 ESTATE PLANNING 36 (June 2011).

Each of these problems can be addressed through the use of disclaimers.

The problems relating to the temporary nature of the 2010 Act are fairly obvious. If the $5 million exemption reverts to $1 million in 2013 and stays that way, married couples who are together worth more than $2 million but less than $10 million may find themselves subject to estate tax at the second spouse's death after 2012 that they would not have had to pay before. As a result, they may not have adequate estate planning in place (specifically, their documents might contain outright gifts to one another, relying on both the higher exemption amount and portability to avoid a federal estate tax liability).

Further, even if the federal tax regime doesn't change after 2012, there is still the problem of state inheritance or estate taxes. After the state death tax credit was eliminated by the 2001 Tax Act, the states responded in very different ways. Some simply eliminated their estate taxes. Others implemented new taxes. To make matters worse, these laws are subject to almost constant revision as states scramble to find sources of revenue to replace those lost in the 2008 recession.

Both of these challenges can be met with disclaimer planning. By creating a disclaimer credit shelter trust, the couple can put off until the first spouse's death the question of whether such a trust is appropriate in their planning. If the exemption stays at the $5 million level and if portability is retained permanently, such a trust may not be necessary for federal tax purposes, and the surviving spouse would have to decide only whether it would be useful for state inheritance or estate tax purposes. On the other hand, if Congress allows the 2010 Act provisions to lapse and the tax law to revert to pre-2001 levels, the surviving spouse can create the shelter trust by disclaiming.

8 USING DISCLAIMERS FOR CREDIT SHELTER DRAFTING AND REPAIRS

A critical use for disclaimers is the preservation of the "credit shelter" amount from estate taxes under Section 2010. This can happen as an affirmative planning tool in the drafting of estate planning documents, or as the solution to estate planning documents that have not contemplated any credit shelter use. Note that the following discussion focuses on techniques other than disclaimers. This is necessary to evaluate the benefits of disclaimer planning relative to the other options.

A. Credit Shelter Drafting with Disclaimers

The 2001 Tax Relief Act, which changed the applicable credit amount, has created disruption in the drafting of the credit shelter (or bypass) trust in two different ways. First, it can alter significantly an estate plan's dispositive provisions. Many married couples have plans that contain shelter trusts for the primary benefit of the couple's children, funded with the applicable exclusion amount, which they assumed would be anywhere from $600,000 (the amount available before 1997) to $3.5 million (the amount available in 2009). After the at least temporary increase to $5 million from the 2010 Act, a larger portion of the predeceased spouse's assets might pass to the credit shelter trust than was intended (assuming portability was not used or available).

This problem can be cured in a couple of different ways. First, the surviving spouse can be the beneficiary of the shelter trust, rather than the children. Second, the gift of the applicable exclusion amount can be divided into two shares, one for the children that is capped at a dollar amount and a second (holding the balance) that passes to a trust of which the surviving spouse is the beneficiary. Obviously, adopting either solution may require a lawyer to notify clients to discuss such changes.

The second problem isn't so easily solved. Many wills and trusts use pecuniary gifts to fund trusts that, if a marital deduction is involved, are affected by the requirements of Rev. Proc. 64-19.[1] Pecuniary testamentary gifts can be funded using either date of death or date of distribution values. If the former, the assets distributed between the qualified terminable interest property (QTIP) and shelter trust shares must be fairly representative of all appreciation and depreciation in the estate. Because of the serious limitations of that method (including lack of asset choice in allocations and administrative cost of making the "fairly representative" calculation),[2] many trusts are funded using distribution values. However, if those values are used and the pecuniary gift is funded with assets that have appreciated between the date of death and the date of funding, gain is triggered on the transfer.[3] This problem could be managed when the gift was $600,000 or less, but it is far more difficult at $5 million. If all of the estate assets have appreci-

1. 1964-1 C.B. 682.

2. *See* Pennell, *Funding Marital Deduction (and other) Bequests*, 35 U. MIAMI PHILIP E. HECKERLING INST. ON EST. PLAN., Ch. 15 (2001).

3. Treas. Reg. § 1.661(a)-2(f)(1).

ated since the date of death, funding such a gift could result in a large income tax liability.

There are four popular solutions to these problems: (1) fractional formula with non pro rata (or "pick and choose") funding; (2) disclaimer shelter trusts; (3) partial QTIP elections; and (4) the "Clayton" QTIP (a variation on partial QTIP elections).

1. Fractional Formula with Pick-and-Choose Funding

Here, the shelter and marital gifts are expressed as a fraction of the residue. This approach solves both problems posed by the 2010 Act. First, no gain or loss is recognized on funding because both share ratably in the post-death appreciation or depreciation. Second, by using three trusts the predeceased spouse still can create a trust for the benefit of children or other beneficiaries, subject to a capped amount (e.g., the lesser of the applicable exclusion amount or $1 million); a second shelter trust for the spouse's benefit to hold the difference (if any) between the applicable exclusion amount and the amount passing to the trustee of the first shelter trust; and a QTIP trust. Of course, this three-trust structure also can be created with pecuniary gifts, but they cannot avoid the potential income tax problem.

The drawback to the fractional formula is the funding: a true fractional formula requires each trust to receive a pro rata share of every asset. This asset division is time consuming, inflexible, and in some cases impossible to achieve. The solution is to give the trustee or executor the discretion to select the assets used to fund each gift, the so called pick-and-choose approach. The problem with that approach is that the IRS could deem it to be a pro rata allocation of assets to each gift, followed by an exchange of assets. Such an exchange would generate capital gains tax liability if the assets had increased in value since the date of death.

There are two relevant Revenue Rulings, a Supreme Court case, and a large number of private rulings dealing with this issue. In 1956 the Internal Revenue Service (IRS) ruled[4] that a partition of

4. Rev. Rul. 56-437, 1956-2 C.B. 507.

joint tenancy property, following which the joint tenants have different interests, is a nontaxable transaction. However, in 1969 the IRS ruled[5] that a non–pro rata division of trust assets between two trust beneficiaries is treated as a pro rata division of the assets, followed by a taxable exchange between the beneficiaries if neither state law nor the governing instrument grants the authority to make such a division. In 1991, the U.S. Supreme Court held[6] that a swap of participation interests in home mortgage loans resulted in realized losses because the interests following the swap were "materially different" from those held before.

Finally, the IRS has issued many favorable private rulings (at least fourteen) in this area in the past few years.[7] Therefore, it is almost certain that fractional formula shelter and QTIP trust gifts can be funded non–pro rata without income tax consequence, so long as either state law or the governing instrument permits it. However, as the IRS delights in reminding us, private rulings can be relied upon only by the taxpayers who request them. The IRS can change its mind in any given situation and find that a capital gain tax liability is incurred in a non–pro rata funding.

2. Disclaimer Shelter Trust

A common client profile is the younger professional couple that has a combined net worth of $2 to $5 million, including a house, retirement plans, and life insurance proceeds. Because these clients may not need estate tax planning in the future, they might each give everything outright to the other, but also provide that if the surviving spouse disclaims a portion of the predeceased spouse's estate, that disclaimed portion passes to a shelter trust. Estate tax uncertainty makes such planning look even more attractive. However, many practitioners do not use disclaimers in planning because they carry the significant risk that one of the disclaimer tests will not be met, and the plan will fail.

5. Rev. Rul. 69-486, 1969-2 C.B. 159.
6. Cottage Savings Ass'n v. Comm'r, 499 U.S. 554 (1991).
7. For an excellent summary, *see* Pennell, *supra* note 2, § 1504.4 n.334.

3. Partial QTIP Election

Even if a trust meets the qualified terminable interest property (QTIP) requirements under Code Section 2056(b)(7), a trustee or executor need not elect such treatment for the entire trust. Any nonelected portion of the trust will first use up any available Section 2010 credit and then generate an estate tax liability. The deceased spouse's will or trust leaves the entire estate to a QTIP trust. After the spouse's death, the executor or trustee decides whether to elect QTIP treatment for the entire trust, or merely a portion of it. If only a partial election is made, a single trust "may be divided into separate trusts to reflect that a partial election has been made."[8] If two trusts are created, the assets must be divided "on a fractional or percentage basis."[9] In other words, the executor or trustee can achieve essentially the same result through partial election that a surviving spouse can through disclaimer.

Partial QTIP election allows for the postmortem determination of whether to create a shelter trust, but does not rely on a disclaimer that must satisfy the requirements described above, so it probably is more reliable than a disclaimer (although poor 706 preparation can still spoil the arrangement). On the other hand, assets must be divided on a fractional or percentage basis. Non–pro rata funding should be available if the logic of the non–pro rata distribution rulings for fractional formulas holds. Further, the two trusts will be identical in terms, so there is no flexibility in drafting as there is with a disclaimer.

4. Clayton QTIP Trust

For years, lawyers theorized that an executor or trustee could alter an estate plan's structure through the QTIP election following the first spouse's death. All of the deceased spouse's assets pass to a QTIP trust for the surviving spouse; but to the extent that the QTIP treatment was not elected for a given asset, it would pass to a different trust that may or may not be for the benefit of the surviving spouse. For years, the IRS challenged this plan. However,

8. Treas. Reg. § 20.2056(b)-7(b)(2)(ii)(A).
9. Treas. Reg. § 20.2056(b)-7(b)(2)(ii)(B).

after several court defeats, most notably in the *Clayton*[10] case, the IRS issued regulations[11] allowing the technique (provided certain requirements are met).

The Clayton QTIP plan has all of the same advantages of the partial QTIP election: postmortem funding decisions, no capital gains tax on funding, and no concerns about whether the surviving spouse has met the disclaimer requirements. The Clayton QTIP has one extra advantage: the property over which no QTIP election is made can pass to a trust with different terms and beneficiaries than the QTIP trust (for instance, to a trust for the benefit of children).

The Clayton QTIP has two drawbacks. First, the spouse probably cannot be the fiduciary making the QTIP election, because the IRS might find that the power was a power of appointment under Sections 2041 and 2514. Second, the Section 2013 credit on previously taxed property (discussed below) may not be available if the trust for which no QTIP election is made is intentionally overfunded to generate an estate tax liability, because the interest in the trust generating the tax is created by later actions by the executor or trustee and therefore cannot be valued at the date of death.[12] Although several commentators have posited this result, neither the IRS nor any court appears to have ruled on it. Obviously, if, as a result of the nonelection, property passed to a trust that created beneficial interests incapable of valuation, no credit would be allowable. However, since the credit is available in the case of partial QTIP elections, there is no theoretical reason why it should not also be available for Clayton QTIPs, because each relies on postmortem decisions not in place as of the date of death. Finally, as with partial QTIP elections, it is not entirely clear that non–pro rata allocations can be made on funding.

---

10. Est. of Clayton v. Commissioner, 976 F.2d 1486 (5th Cir. 1992).
11. Treas. Reg. § 20.2056(b)-7(d)(3)(i).
12. *See* Kalter & Newman, *Tax Court Changes Position as to Certain Contingent QTIP Elections*, Estate Planning, June 1996.

5. Comparing Funding Methods

Each technique has advantages and disadvantages. Perhaps the best choice may be a combination of techniques. For example, a married client's estate plan may provide that all of her assets pass to Trust A for the benefit of her husband and that Trust A qualifies for QTIP treatment. If, upon her death, her trustee or executor does not elect QTIP over a portion of the trust, then the non-elected portion passes to Trust B. Finally, if her husband disclaims any assets, they pass to Trust C. This provides a great deal of flexibility. For instance, Trust A could be a standard QTIP trust; Trust B (the Clayton trust) could be the shelter trust and may have as beneficiaries the husband and the children; and Trust C could give the husband an income interest capable of valuation, so that any estate tax attributable to this trust would qualify for the previously taxed property credit. The husband upon the wife's death could decide whether to use the fractional or percentage funding of the Clayton QTIP or instead fund with specific assets by disclaiming them. Finally, if the husband accidentally violates one of the disclaimer rules, he has not automatically eliminated the possibility of creating a shelter trust, because Trust B can serve that purpose.

This combination has at least one problem in addition to its complexity. There is the slight chance that the disclaimer will not be qualified if the surviving spouse as executor also has the power to change the trust structure through the QTIP election. The regulations provide that, if a will divides the residue in thirds, all of which pass to a single beneficiary, and the will also provides that each third goes to a different beneficiary in the event of disclaimer, the disclaimers will not be qualified.[13] The disclaiming beneficiary is given through this method the ability to direct where a third of the residue is to pass. On the other hand, a beneficiary can be given the ability to disclaim specific assets in favor of different beneficiaries.[14]

13. Treas. Reg. § 25.2518-2(e)(5), Ex. 9.
14. Treas. Reg. § 25.2518-2(e)(5), Ex. 10.

B. Credit Shelter Repairs

The bypass or credit shelter trust, of course, is designed to "shelter" from the estate of the surviving spouse the estate tax-free portion of the deceased spouse's estate, and it generally is funded with the amount of the available unified credit or applicable exclusion amount. A disclaimer can sometimes be used when the estate planning documents do not provide for such a trust. In an Arkansas case, decided before the unlimited marital deduction was available, a disclaimer fixed two errors.[15] The decedent left his entire estate to his wife, failing to mention their two adult children. As pretermitted heirs, they were entitled to the entire estate as their intestate share, subject only to the wife's dower and homestead rights. The two children filed an "election and disclaimer," each electing to take his "full intestate share, reduced by an amount equal to one-half of the maximum marital deduction (after considering all property passing to the surviving spouse, whether outside or under the decedent's will)." Their disclaimers were qualified, and the estate was entitled to the maximum marital deduction, with the balance passing to the next generation, subject only to tax on the father's estate and not to tax on the mother's estate.

Beneficiaries can use disclaimers to do their own estate planning. For example, a trust beneficiary can disclaim a general power of appointment to ensure that the trust property will not be included in his own gross estate under Section 2041,[16] or to eliminate other powers over a trust that might produce adverse transfer tax consequences to him or his estate.[17] In some other examples:

---

15. PLR 8145036.

16. *See, e.g.*, PLRs 8824014, 8721012, and 8603030; TAM 8523010.

17. PLR 8122075. *See* Rev. Rul. 79-353, 1979-2 C.B. 325. The IRS's revocation of Rev. Rul. 79-353 in Rev. Rul. 95-58, 1995-2 C.B. 191, eliminated the need to disclaim any power to replace a corporate trustee with a new corporate trustee. As a result of Rev. Rul. 95-58, the retention of such a power will not result in the inclusion of the trust property in the power holder's estate under § 2036 or 2038.

- Parents disclaimed a portion of their deceased son's intestate estate, which therefore passed to their other children;[18]
- A decedent's brother disclaimed almost all of his share of the decedent's estate so it could pass to the disclaimant's issue;[19]
- A son disclaimed a bequest of his deceased parent's residuary estate, which therefore fell into a standby trust that the parent's will had provided for the son's children in the event that the son did disclaim;[20] and
- A whole family of youngsters retained their right to receive trust income, under the terms of the trust, for 21 years after the death of their parent, the first income beneficiary, but disclaimed their contingent interest in the trust principal that would have been distributable to them at the end of the twenty-one-year period.[21]

To decrease the burden of double estate taxes when a distributee's death follows close upon the donor's death, the estate planning for the second estate can occur even after the second death, if that death follows the first within nine months.[22]

---

18. PLR 8451048.
19. PLR 8647044. *See also* PLR 9001062.
20. PLR 8509092.
21. *See, e.g.*, PLR 8825101 and PLR 8638022.
22. Ferguson v. U.S., 81-1 USTC ¶ 13,409, (D. Ariz. 1981). *But see* Fleming Est. v. Comr., 58 T.C.M. 1034 (1989), *aff'd*, 974 F.2d 894 (7th Cir. 1992) (husband died 9/23/83 with will leaving everything to wife; wife died 5/13/84; son, as executor of second estate, executed disclaimer 7/19/84. Disclaimer was held to be untimely; the nine months started on date of husband's death, not, as wife's estate contended, on date of probate of husband's will).

MORE SOPHISTICATED TAX DISCLAIMER TECHNIQUES

9

As with all other estate and gift tax planning techniques, disclaimers can be used in fairly complex ways. What follows is a very general overview of some of those techniques.

A. Formula Disclaimers

A disclaimer of a specific pecuniary amount out of a bequest or gift is not qualified unless "no income or other benefit of the disclaimed amount" inures to the disclaimant's benefit.[1] When making such a pecuniary, or formula, disclaimer, the amount disclaimed "and any income attributable to such amount" must be segregated based on "the fair market value of the assets on the date of the disclaimer or on a basis that is fairly representative of value changes." The regulations provide an example of a qualified fractional

1. Treas. Reg. § 25.2518-3(c).

disclaimer.[2] Formula disclaimers are useful when a surviving spouse wants to disclaim only enough to fully use up the predeceased spouse's applicable exclusion amount under Section 2010, and the sole asset of the predeceased spouse's estate is hard to value. The surviving spouse can disclaim a fraction of the asset, the numerator of which is the amount that can be sheltered by the unified credit and the denominator of which is the asset's value as finally determined for estate tax purposes.

Many private letter rulings illustrate the use of a reduce-to-zero formula where the surviving spouse executes a qualified disclaimer to reduce the overfunded marital deduction bequest.[3] Several rulings illustrate the use of a unified credit carve-out formula or other formulae designed to preserve the unified credit shelter amount for children who disclaim their interests in order to benefit their surviving parent and to obtain or increase the marital deduction.[4]

This strategy also may be helpful in disclaiming "discounted" assets (such as family limited liability companies or fractional interests in real property). For example, assume that (1) a donor wants to give $13,000 worth of stock in Company A to her daughter; (2) the donor wants this gift to qualify for annual exclusion treatment under Section 2503; and (3) the donor has used up all of her exemption amount for gifts, so any gift in excess of $13,000 to her daughter will generate a gift tax liability. Also assume that Company A is a closely held and hard-to-value company. The donor can execute a transfer document stating that the donor gives *X* number of shares to daughter; but if daughter disclaims any portion of this gift, then the disclaimed portion passes to Charity B. The daughter then executes a disclaimer, under which she disclaims a number of shares equal to a fraction of the total, the numerator of which is the fair market value of the stock on the date of transfer as finally determined for federal gift tax purposes reduced by $13,000, and the denominator of which is the value of all the shares on the date of transfer (again, as finally determined for federal transfer tax

2. *Id.*, Ex. 20.
3. *See, e.g.*, PLR 8702023, PLR 8637108, and PLR 8624066.
4. *See, e.g.*, TAM 8639002; PLR 8514095.

purposes). If the value of the gift is challenged, any excess value ought to pass to charity, resulting in a charitable deduction and therefore no taxable gift from the donor to her daughter.

This technique has been the subject of several articles.[5] If it works, it creates greater certainty for the taxpayer that, regardless of an audit, no additional transfer taxes would be due (although the client certainly needs legitimate charitable intent, because some of the stock could and probably should actually go to the charity). Unfortunately, the Internal Revenue Service (IRS) used several early cases[6] in technical advice memoranda, under which the IRS invalidated "value definition" clauses.[7]

However, in recent years the courts have looked much more favorably on this technique. The tax court found a "value definition" clause wanting in the *McCord v. Commissioner* case,[8] but only because it did not refer to the value "as finally determined" for gift tax purposes. The most important case for disclaimers in this area is the *Christiansen v. Commissioner* case.[9] This case (already discussed for other reasons in Chapter 5) dealt with a decedent's will that left the decedent's entire estate to her daughter, provided that any property the daughter disclaimed was to pass in part to a charitable lead trust and the balance outright to charity. The charitable trust lasted for twenty years, with the remainder interest passing to daughter. Daughter made a formula disclaimer of her outright gift, phrased as follows:

> Intending to disclaim a fractional portion of the Gift, [daughter] hereby disclaims that portion of the gift determined by reference to a fraction, the numerator of which is the fair market value of the Gift (before payment of debts, expenses and taxes) on April 17, 2001, less Six Million Three Hundred Thousand and No/100 Dollars

5. *See, e.g.*, McCaffrey, *Tax Tuning the Estate by Formula*, 33rd ANN. PHILIP E. HECKERLING INST. ON EST. PLAN. (2002).

6. *See, e.g.*, Comm'r v. Procter, 142 F.2d 824 (4th Cir. 1944), *cert. denied*, 323 U.S. 756 (1944); Est. of McLendon v. Comm'r, T.C. Memo 1993-459.

7. *See, e.g.*, TAM 200225023 and TAM 200337012.

8. 120 T.C. 358 (2003).

9. 130 T.C. 1 (2008).

> ($6,300,000.00) and the denominator of which is the fair market value of the Gift (before payment of debts, expenses and taxes on April 17, 2001 (the "Disclaimed Portion"). For purposes of this paragraph, the fair market value of the Gift (before payment of debts, expenses and taxes on April 17, 2001, shall be the price at which the Gift (before payment of debts, expenses and taxes) would have changed hands on April 17, 2001, between a hypothetical willing buyer and a hypothetical willing seller, neither being under any compulsion to buy or sell and both having reasonable knowledge of relevant facts for purposes of Chapter 11 of the [Internal Revenue] Code, as such value is finally determined for federal estate tax purposes.

April 17, 2001, was the date of the decedent's death; and $6,300,000 was the amount the daughter and her advisors determined that the daughter and her family, as well as the family business, would need for their future. The disclaimer also contained the following savings clause, which provided that

> to the extent that the disclaimer set forth above in this instrument is not effective to make it a qualified disclaimer, [daughter] hereby takes such actions to the extent necessary to make the disclaimer set forth above a qualified disclaimer within the meaning of section 2518 of the Code.[10]

As an initial matter, the court noted that

> if one took an especially skeptical view of the situation, the final quoted phrase in the disclaimer and the savings clause meant that the Commissioner would face an interesting choice if he thought the estate was lowballing its own value—any success in increasing the value of the estate might only increase the charitable deduction that the estate would claim. Which would presumably reduce

10. *Id.* at 5.

> the incentive of the Commissioner to challenge the value that the estate claimed for itself.[11]

And that is more or less the argument the IRS made. The court also noted, however, that the overall estate plan contained a legitimate charitable goal, and that the court was to look only at the legal consequences of the documents, not the factual issue of the motivation behind them.[12]

The IRS made two specific arguments against the application of the formula clause: (1) an increase in the amount of the charitable deduction by application of the formula upon a redetermination of value was contingent on a condition subsequent; and (2) the adjustment phrase in the disclaimer (that the fraction was to be calculated based on values as "finally determined for federal estate tax purposes") was void as against public policy. The court rejected both arguments. First, the transfer in this case (and unlike that in *Procter*) was not contingent on any event that occurred after the decedent's death; it remained 25 percent of the value of the estate in excess of $6,300,000. The argument between the IRS and the decedent's estate as to asset value does not make the transfer itself contingent. The court also distinguished *Procter* in rejecting the IRS's public policy argument: there, the proposed adjustment would have undone a transfer, whereas here, only a reallocation of property would have occurred. For these reasons, the court allowed an increased charitable deduction as a result of the increase in the asset value of the decedent's estate following the IRS audit.

After *Christiansen*, the Ninth Circuit also upheld the use of defined value clauses (though not in the disclaimer context).[13] In *Petter*, the decedent during her lifetime transferred by gift interests in a family limited liability company (LLC) equal to her unused gift tax exemption and 10 percent of the value the trust would ultimately hold. Three days later, she sold the remaining 90 percent of what would be the trust's total LLC interests. Both transfers were

11. *Id.* at 6.
12. *Id.*
13. Est. of Petter v. Comm'r, 108 A.F.T.R. 2d 2011.

coupled with simultaneous donations of LLC units to two public charities. In a footnote, the court noted that this was a "charitable freeze," one that sought "to ensure that if the IRS successfully challenges a taxpayer's valuation of a gift, the amount by which the gift was undervalued does not go to the IRS . . ."[14]

The gift assignment assigned to the trust as a gift

> The number of Units . . . that equals one-half the [maximum] dollar amount that can pass free of federal gift tax by reason of Transferor's applicable exclusion amount allowed by Code Section 2010(c) [and] assigns to [the charity] as a gift . . . the difference between the total number of Units . . . and the number of Units assigned to the Trust.

It went on to provide that if the value for the units as finally determined for federal gift tax purposes exceeded the amount above, the trustee agreed to transfer the excess units to the charity. Further, the charity agreed to give back any units if the value for gift purposes was less than the stated amount. The sale documents contained similar provisions. Based upon the appraised value, the charities received 1,867.38 units, and the trusts received 8,465.31 units. The decedent filed a Form 709, reporting the transaction and claiming no tax due.

The IRS on audit challenged the appraised value. The taxpayer agreed to the increased value, and the trustee transferred additional units to the charity. However, the IRS also claimed the formula clauses were void as against public policy, which meant that the adjusted value of the initial transfer to the trusts over the appraised value was a taxable gift with no offsetting charitable deduction. As a result, it issued a notice of deficiency for over $2 million.

In reviewing the matter, the court noted the basis for review: a finding of whether the formula clauses created a "condition precedent" that would render the clauses void. The court noted that the transfers were effective immediately upon execution of the

14. *Id.* at fn. 2.

transfer documents and delivery of the units; "the only possible open question was the value of the units transferred, not the transfers themselves." The IRS argued that, because the charities would not have received the additional amounts but for the IRS audit, the audit became a condition precedent. The court rejected this argument, relying in part on *Christiansen* and *McCord.* As a result, the court sided with the taxpayer, granting the additional charitable deduction for the transfers made by the trustee to the charities after the audit.

Although this case does not involve disclaimers, it does point the way for a planning opportunity.[15] Testamentary gifts could be constructed to leave hard-to-value assets to an heir, with any disclaimed assets passing to a charity. The heir could then disclaim a formula amount in a manner similar to that in *Petter.* If such a technique is used, however, the disclaimant should be prepared to disclaim a proportion that will result in some assets passing to charity. Although this was not stated overtly in the decision, the court may have been persuaded in part by the fact that the charities actually received substantial gifts before the audit.

Caution is still required when using these clauses. In several cases, there were flaws in the way that the gift was constructed. Further, the regulations under Section 2518 permit disclaimers that are described in terms of a fractional share.[16] Therefore, the disclaimer approach to defined value gifts may be more effective than defining the gift according to the fraction when it is made, which was the case in the situations described above. In any event, great caution must be used when adopting such a technique, and full disclosure of the risks must be made to the client in advance. Finally, the taxpayer-friendly cases all involved increased gifts to charity as a result of the audit, so genuine charitable intent at this point is important.

15. For an additional description of planning opportunities using these clauses, and a description of the distinctions between the different approaches, *see* Dwyer & Ramirez, *Estate Planning by the Numbers—Defined-Value and Other Formula Transfers*, 37 EST. PLAN. J. 11 (May 2010).

16. Treas. Reg. § 25.2518-3(d), Ex. 18 and 19.

B. Intentionally Creating an Estate Tax (or Using Exemption)

Rather than being used to maximize a marital deduction, disclaimers can be used to reduce it so that some estate tax is paid upon the first spouse's death. The reason for doing this, of course, used to be to take advantage of the predeceased spouse's lower estate tax brackets, rather than passing all of property in excess of the applicable exclusion amount to the surviving spouse, so that it is taxed at the highest rate in her estate. At the time of this writing, it is unclear whether the transfer taxes will continue to exist, and even if they do, whether they will adopt a graduated rate as they did in the past. Finally, as any experienced estate planner will tell you, clients will not pay taxes early. However, the technique may have some enduring use in the area of the previously taxed property credit, described below.

C. Using the Previously Taxed Property Credit

Section 2013 states that the estate tax "shall be credited with all or part of the amount of the federal estate tax paid with respect to the transfer of property . . . to the decedent by or from a person . . . who died within 10 years before, or within 2 years after, the decedent's death." This credit (the "previously taxed property credit") equals 100 percent of the estate tax previously paid if the decedent died within 2 years of the person whose estate previously paid the tax, 80 percent if the decedent died within 4 years, 60 percent if the decedent died within 6 years, 40 percent if the decedent died within 8 years, and 20 percent if the decedent died within 10 years. Calculating the credit is quite complicated.[17]

---

17. For more details, *see* Herrmann, *Planning for Use of the TPT Credit Yields Significant Tax Savings*, 28 Estate Planning 478 (October 2001).

1. Planning with the Previously Taxed Property Credit

The credit can create significant estate tax savings under limited circumstances. It is available in a decedent's estate even for tax paid on property that is not includable in that estate if the decedent was the beneficiary of a trust, the corpus of which was previously subjected to estate tax liability. The credit calculation assumes the decedent lived to her actuarial life expectancy and received all appropriate trust distributions, whether or not she actually did. Further, because the credit is based upon the amount of tax paid at the first spouse's death, a larger credit can be generated in the second spouse's estate if estate taxes are paid in the first spouse's estate on property passing to other beneficiaries. The additional tax paid in the first spouse's estate increases his marginal rate and therefore increases the credit.

To obtain the benefit of this credit, however, three things must happen. First, estate tax must be paid at the first spouse's death, even if the estate plan as originally drafted contemplated the maximum use of the marital deduction. Although such early payment can create greater tax savings for the couple's children,[18] many clients do not want to incur estate tax liability any earlier than they have to. Second, the surviving spouse must have a trust interest capable of valuation. This would include trusts that give the spouse all net income annually. However, if the spouse is only one of several beneficiaries of a pot trust, distributions from which are in the discretion of a trustee, the interest probably is not capable of being valued, because although at least one court case[19] has approved the use of the credit for a discretionary interest in a trust, at least two private rulings[20] have disallowed such use. Third, regulations[21] prohibit the use of the standard actuarial tables in determining the surviving spouse's interest if that spouse

18. *See, e.g.*, Pennell & Williamson, *The Economics of Prepaying Wealth Transfer Tax*, TRUSTS & ESTATES (June–Aug. 1997; published in three installments).

19. Est. of Weinstein v. U.S., 820 F.2d 201 (6th Cir. 1987).

20. TAMs 8717006 and 8944005.

21. Treas. Reg. § 20.7520-3(b)(3).

is terminally ill (which is defined as a deteriorating physical condition creating at least a 50 percent probability of death within one year). Simultaneous death also may preclude the use of the credit.[22]

Trust drafting, obviously, is very important here; in addition to giving the surviving spouse an interest that is capable of valuation, the document also should not give the trustee the power to alter the value of that interest (like the power to allocate between income and principal in a manner inconsistent with state law). Such powers have been found to defeat the use of the previously-taxed property (PTP) credit and the "annual exclusion" for gift tax purposes under Section 2503(b).[23] The trustee also should not have the power to invest in non-income-producing property.[24] However, the surviving spouse can have a noncumulative annual power to withdraw 5 percent of the trust principal.[25]

2. Using Disclaimers to Create a Previously Taxed Property Credit

Disclaimer planning often proves useful when taking advantage of the previously taxed property credit. Assume two elderly spouses die within a few months of each other. The first spouse leaves all of his property in a shelter trust and a qualified terminable interest property (QTIP) trust for the survivor. Assume also that the predeceased spouse had a large independent retirement account (IRA), the beneficiary designation of which named first the spouse and then the couple's children as beneficiaries. Following the survivor's death, her personal representative can disclaim a portion of the QTIP trust, generating estate tax liability in the predeceased spouse's estate and allowing for the possible use of the credit for tax on prior transfers. Her personal representative also can

22. *See, e.g.*, Est. of Harrison v. Commissioner, 115 T.C. No. 13 (2000); Carter v. U.S., 921 F.2d 63 (5th Cir. 1991); Est. of Marks v. Commissioner, 94 T.C. 720 (1990).
23. Rev. Rul. 76-275, 1976-2 C.B. 299; Holbrook v. United States, 575 F.2d 1288 (9th Cir. 1978); VanDen Weymelenberg v. United States, 397 F.2d 443 (7th Cir. 1968).
24. *See, e.g.*, Treas. Reg. § 25.7520-3(b).
25. Rev. Rul. 79-211, 1979-2 C.B. 319; Est. of Shapiro, 66 T.C.M. 1067 (1993).

disclaim her interest (assuming she has not taken any benefits) in the IRA. The IRA property is distributable to the children, causing a larger tax to be paid in the predeceased spouse's estate and increasing the size of the credit.

The uncertain status of the transfer taxes at the time of this writing may render this technique close to useless, because it is counterproductive to intentionally create an estate tax liability at the first spouse's death if there will be no tax due on the second spouse's death as a result of law changes. Further, most of the benefit from the technique comes from taking advantage of graduated rate tables in each spouse's estate. Such tables currently do not exist. The previously taxed property credit was a little-used provision even before the 2010 Act; after it, it may become practically nonexistent. However, practitioners should continue to review carefully the health of a surviving spouse upon the first spouse's death to determine whether postmortem planning for the credit is appropriate.

D. Disclaimers with Retirement Plans and IRAs

As everyone knows, retirement plans and IRAs (here referred to collectively as "plans") are extremely effective retirement savings vehicles because assets grow inside the plan free of income tax liability. Once the participant in the plan reaches her required beginning date (RBD), she must begin making annual withdrawals from the plan, and upon her death, her beneficiary must withdraw all plan assets either within the five-year period beginning with the year in which the participant died (if she died before her RBD), or over her remaining life expectancy (if she died after her RBD). However, if the beneficiary was a "designated beneficiary," that beneficiary can withdraw the assets over the beneficiary's (not the participant's) remaining life expectancy.[26] This additional

26. Code § 401(a)(9)(B).

tax deferral obviously is a huge benefit if the beneficiary is much younger than the participant.

Designated beneficiary, defined as an individual only, is a tax concept.[27] The actual plan beneficiary is the person or entity named in a beneficiary designation or the plan document. This actual beneficiary may or may not qualify as a designated beneficiary. Further, if the participant names several beneficiaries, each must be an individual for the participant to have a designated beneficiary. So, for example, if a participant names her grandchild and her favorite charity as equal beneficiaries of her IRA, there is no designated beneficiary, because one of the actual beneficiaries is not an individual. Therefore, the grandchild would have to withdraw IRA assets (and pay tax on those withdrawals) either within five years or over the participant's life expectancy.

If the surviving spouse is the sole designated beneficiary at the time of the participant's death, the spouse can elect to treat the participant's IRA as the spouse's own by making a "spousal rollover" of the plan assets into an IRA owned by the spouse. The effect of this election is that the spouse can wait until her own RBD before taking out minimum withdrawals, can use the recalculation method for computing her own minimum withdrawals, and can name her own beneficiaries, who in turn will be able to use their own life expectancies if they are designated beneficiaries.[28]

The date for identifying a designated beneficiary is September 30 of the year after the year in which the participant dies, whether or not she has reached her RBD at that time.[29] The participant's designated beneficiary "will be determined based on the beneficiaries designated as of the date of death who remain beneficiaries as of September 30 of the calendar year following the calendar year of the [participant's] death."[30] So the beneficiary must have been

---

27. Treas. Reg. § 1.401(a)(9)-4, Q&A 1.

28. For a complete discussion of the spousal rollover and the issues that can arise, as well as for the answers to all retirement plan related questions, *See* Choate, Life and Death Planning for Retirement Benefits, Ch. 3 (7th ed. 2011).

29. Treas. Reg. § 1.401(a)(9)-4, Q&A 4.

30. Treas. Reg. § 1.401(a)(9)-4, Q&A 4(a).

named as of the date of death *and* must still be around on September 30 of the following year. For example, if the participant's sister and the participant's favorite charity each are named as beneficiary on the date of death, the sister can qualify as designated beneficiary if the charity is given its half of the plan assets before September 30 of the year after the year of the participant's death. This is so because the sister is a beneficiary on the date of death and becomes the sole beneficiary on September 30 of the following year. However, if the participant names as beneficiary her estate, the sole beneficiary of which is the sister, and the plan is distributed to her before September 30 of the following year, then the sister is *not* a designated beneficiary, because although she is the sole beneficiary on the testing date, she was not a named beneficiary as of the date of death.

This means that a beneficiary who either does not qualify for designated beneficiary status (e.g., a charity) or is elderly and not able to obtain significant deferral can be eliminated from the designated beneficiary determination either through disclaimer or through distribution of that beneficiary's entire interest in the plan.

Disclaimers also can be used to defer the question of whether to fund a credit shelter trust with plan assets. Many clients have taxable estate consisting primarily or solely of retirement plan assets and perhaps a personal residence. These clients might want to have a shelter trust at the first spouse's death to protect the deceased spouse's applicable exclusion amount. However, if plan assets pass to a trust rather than to the surviving spouse outright, he trust may not be drafted to qualify its beneficiary (the spouse) as a designated beneficiary; or, if the surviving spouse is considered the designated beneficiary, the plan assets must then be withdrawn over the spouse's life expectancy, as determined in the year of the participant spouse's death. This is more rigid than the rules applicable to the spousal rollover IRA, under which the spouse is allowed to recalculate the spouse's life expectancy in determining the required minimum distribution and following which the remainder beneficiaries, such as the spouse's children, can use their own life expectancies upon the surviving spouse's death.

While the nuances of required minimum distribution rules are beyond the scope of this presentation, the point is that the transfer tax savings of funding the shelter trust will be offset by the loss of income tax benefits if plan assets are used to fund that trust. Further, given the uncertainty of the applicable exclusion amount, it may be that at the time of the deceased spouse's death a shelter trust is unnecessary because the surviving spouse's applicable exclusion is enough to shelter the combined net worth of both spouses.

One way to deal with this problem is to draft the beneficiary designation for the retirement plan assets to leave the plan assets outright to the surviving spouse, but if the surviving spouse disclaims plan assets, to a shelter trust. By including this disclaimer shelter trust plan into the plan beneficiary designation, the surviving spouse is allowed to take a second look at the time of the participant spouse's death in order to determine whether funding a shelter trust with plan assets is the best choice.

Such a plan adds both flexibility and drawbacks. Most important, it doesn't resolve the issue of transfer tax savings versus income tax savings; it just defers it until the first spouse's death. Also, the disclaimer, if made, must meet all of the Section 2518 requirements. However, they are useful. In many rulings,[31] the decedent's estate plan funded a residuary credit shelter trust with two IRAs, but the terms of the trust for whatever reason did not meet the minimum distribution requirements for the IRAs. The surviving spouse and all other beneficiaries disclaimed their interests in the trust, and the decedent's children and grandchildren also disclaimed their intestate interests in the trust property. As a result, the trust property passed to the surviving spouse by intestacy, and she was able to roll over the two IRAs into her own IRA in a tax-free rollover.

There are several other examples of disclaimer planning with retirement plans contained in private rulings:

- A spouse who was the beneficiary of her deceased spouse's IRA disclaimed her interest in the IRA and in her spouse's estate. As a result, the IRA passed to the couple's children,

31. *See, e.g.*, PLR 9615043 and PLR 200447040.

presumably so that they could use their lives as measuring lives for required minimum distribution (RMD) purposes;[32]

- A surviving spouse disclaimed her interest as beneficiary of her predeceased spouse's IRA, with the result that the interest in the IRA passed through the deceased spouse's estate to a family trust. The trust was a "see-through," and the surviving spouse became the measuring life;[33]
- A predeceased spouse named a trust as the beneficiary of his IRA. His surviving spouse disclaimed her interest in the trust, rendering it void. As a result, the IRA passed through the deceased spouse's estate outright to the spouse;[34]
- Deceased spouse's IRA named his children as beneficiary, but they wanted it to benefit their mother. The children disclaimed their interest as beneficiary, so the IRA passed to the deceased spouse's estate, which named as beneficiary a marital and a shelter trust. The executor made a non–pro rata distribution of the retirement plan to the marital trust (pursuant to a power in the will to do so). The surviving spouse as trustee then distributed the entire IRA to herself, pursuant to her power under the trust to make distributions for any reason, and then treated the IRA as her own.[35]

Finally, the IRS in a Revenue Ruling[36] ruled that a disclaimer of an IRA is valid, even when the disclaimant-beneficiary has taken an RMD distribution between the date of the participant's death and the date of the disclaimer. In this situation the RMD is treated as a distribution of corpus, and the beneficiary who has received it can disclaim all but a pro rata share of the income attributable to that RMD payment.[37]

---

32. PLR 200839030.
33. PLR 200522012.
34. PLR 200938042.
35. PLR 200934046.
36. Rev. Rul. 2005-36, 2005-1 C.B. 1368.
37. *See also* PLR 201125009.

E. Disclaiming to Apply Alternate Valuation

With the volatility in the economy, the Section 2032 election (which allows the executor to value the assets as of six months after death rather than on the date of death) is an important tool. It can only be used, however, if the election results in estate tax savings. In a typical plan that reduces transfer tax to zero on the first spouse's death, therefore, the alternate valuation election is not available. However, a disclaimer can be used to generate estate tax on the date of death, and that tax can then be reduced to zero using the alternate valuation election. If the disclaimed property passes to the shelter trust, the disclaimer allows the surviving spouse to "refill" the shelter trust (at least to some extent), making up for the amount in that trust lost to asset depreciation. To do so, the estate planning documents must provide that any property the spouse disclaims passes to the shelter trust (or to a disclaimer trust using similar terms). This approach also might allow use of the previously taxed property credit (discussed above).

F. Disclaimers to Private Foundations

The IRS has privately ruled[38] that a person can disclaim property to a private foundation of which she is a director under the right circumstances. Typically, the disclaimant must have no right to participate in the election or removal of members or directors, the appointment of any committee or directors, or to exercise of any control over the disclaimed property. In this case, the disclaimers will be qualified. This is the opposite conclusion from that in Rev. Rul. 72-552,[39] where a decedent's right to designate entities that would possess property distributable from a corporation of which the decedent was a director and the president resulted in inclusion of the property in the decedent's gross estate under Section 2036.

38. *See, e.g.*, PLR 199929027, PLR 9317039, and PLR 9320008.
39. 1972-2 C.B. 525.

Note that the disclaimant/director's control over the disclaimed assets can be eliminated either by the disclaimant herself also disclaiming such control, or by changing the corporate documents.[40]

G. To Increase or Save the Charitable Deduction

If a testator gives a specific gift to an individual and the residue to charity, the individual beneficiary can (obviously) disclaim to increase the charitable gift. This can come about in indirect ways; for instance, in PLR 200127007 the IRS held that the disclaimer of the benefit conferred by a decedent's waiver of the Section 2207A right of recovery would be a qualified disclaimer if the disclaimer otherwise met the Section 2518 requirements and that the resulting increase in the value of property passing to charity would qualify for the charitable deduction.

Disclaimers also can be used to save charitable deductions for decedents' estates.[41] For instance, disclaimers can be used as part of a "qualified reformation" of a charitable remainder trust that has been improperly drafted, saving the charitable deduction for income, estate, and gift tax purposes. For an interest to be "reform-

40. *See, e.g.*, PLR 200802010, PLR 200744005, and PLR 199944038.

41. Jaecker Est. v. Comr., 58 T.C. 166 (1972), *acq.*, 1974-1 C.B. 2 (Will of decedent who died in 1964 provided for trust, with income payable to A, B, and C, and remainder payable at death of survivor of A, B, and C to named charities. The trustees were given discretionary power to invade corpus for the care and comfort of A, B, and C and were given administrative powers to allocate receipts to principal or income. The disclaimers of A, B, and C with respect to the "care and comfort" power and with respect to the discretionary administrative power, to ensure that they would receive no income in excess of the amount that state law would permit absent such power, made the value of the charitable remainder ascertainable and therefore deductible.). *See also* PLR 200052006 (decedent's estate entitled to charitable deduction for interests in trust, individual retirement account, and annuity contracts passing to charity as result of qualified disclaimers).

able," certain technical requirements must be met.[42] For instance, a decedent's 1980 will bequeathed 25 percent of his residuary estate in the form of an obsolete charitable trust, with income to A, B, and C and remainder to charity. The trustees were given the power to pay the expenses of the last illness and funeral of A, B, and C from the trust income or corpus. The qualified disclaimer by A, B, and C of their interest in the trust principal permitted the reformation of the trust into a deductible charitable remainder trust.[43]

Disclaimers can be used in some cases specifically to save charitable remainder trusts. The IRS privately approved[44] a trust reformation designed to qualify the trust as a charitable remainder unitrust (CRUT), where the first step in the process was a disclaimer. In this case, the decedent established a testamentary trust that was to pay son 50 percent of the trust income; principal for comfort, maintenance, and support; and under a separate provision, medical expenses. At the end of ten years, the son was entitled to 50 percent of the trust principal outright; the balance was to be held in trust, with discretionary principal available for the medical expenses only, and the remainder was distributable at son's death to four charities. Clearly not qualifying for a charitable deduction, the trust was reformed by dividing it into two trusts: 50 percent passed to trust A, which lasted for only ten years, and the balance passed to trust B, which was then to be reformed into a CRUT. However, before the division into two trusts, the son disclaimed his right to receive principal for medical expenses, which otherwise would have lasted for the duration of the trust and would have disqualified it as a CRUT.

Although not stated in the ruling, the disclaimer was required as part of the process because, if the principal invasion power had simply been eliminated as part of the reformation, it could have had adverse gift tax consequences. By consenting to the reformation, the son willingly would have given up a right to principal in favor of the charity. However, because it would not have passed

42. §§ 2055(e)(3), 2522(c)(4).

43. PLR 8550018. *See also* PLR 9004011, PLR 7821045, PLR 9347013, PLR 9532026; and PLR 200010019.

44. PLR 200535006.

outright to the charity, it would not have qualified for a gift tax charitable deduction.

H. Special Use Valuation Purposes

Section 2032A permits special use valuation, for federal estate tax purposes, of certain farmland and other qualified real property that constitute the required percentage amount of a decedent's estate.[45] If a Section 2032A election is made, the land is valued not at its highest and best use value, but at its value as farmland or other qualified use.[46] To qualify for this election, the real property must pass to a qualified heir;[47] must have been used in a qualified manner for 5 of the 8 years up to the decedent's death,[48] and must, for 10 years or, if earlier, the death of qualified the heir, continue to be used in a qualified manner and held by a qualified heir or members of his or her family.[49] Qualified heir is limited to ancestor, spouse, lineal descendant, lineal descendant of a spouse or of a parent, or spouse of any such lineal descendant.[50]

Disclaimers can direct qualified property to pass only to qualified heirs. For example, a qualified heir disclaimed his ability to appoint the remainder in qualified property to nonqualified appointees. The executor was therefore permitted to elect special use valuation.[51] However, the qualified disclaimer requirements must be followed for this technique to work; in the case of a qualified heir who disclaimed a power of appointment over qualified property, but only to the extent the power would permit him to appoint the property to any person who was not a "qualified heir," did not make a qualified disclaimer. Disclaiming "only certain rights with respect to the power while retaining others" does not

45. § 2032A(b)(1)(A), (B).
46. § 2032A(a)(1).
47. §§ 2032A(b)(1), 2032A(c)(1).
48. § 2032A(b)(1).
49. § 2032A(c).
50. § 2032A(e)(1), (2).
51. Rev. Rul. 82-140, 1982-2 C.B. 208.

result in a qualified disclaimer.[52] The ruling did not state who the takers in default of exercise of the appointment were. If they were the son's issue or other qualified heirs, and the son had disclaimed the power, rather than cut it down or rewritten it, Section 2032A election would have been permitted.

There can be other traps for the unwary in the use of a disclaimer with respect to Section 2032A property. For instance, each person who has an interest in the special use valuation property must sign a written recapture agreement consenting to the collection of this tax[53] that is filed with a timely filed federal estate tax return. So, where a wife disclaimed her interest in special use property included in her husband's estate so that it passed to their three children, but only she signed the recapture agreement, the IRS and the tax court refused to give effect to the special use valuation election.[54]

I. Altering the Estate Plan to Collapse Trusts

Disclaimers can be used to change an estate plan by collapsing trusts under state law. For example, a life tenant might make a timely disclaimer of his life estate, accelerating the remainder and causing it to be paid as of the testator's death.[55] This was the case for a grandfather named as the sole current beneficiary of a discretionary trust that left the balance of the trust property in further trust for his grandchildren at his death. The grandfather, who did not need discretionary trust distributions, disclaimed his trust interest, resulting in the grandchildren's trust being funded immediately.[56]

52. TAM 8146020.

53. § 2032A(d).

54. McDonald v. Comr., 89 T.C. 293 (1987), *aff'd on this issue, rev'd on another*, 853 F.2d 1494 (8th Cir. 1988), *op. on remand*, 56 T.C.M. 1598 (1989).

55. Pate v. Ford, 297 S.C. 294, 376 S.E.2d 775 (1989), *rev'g* 293 S.C. 268, 360 S.E.2d 145 (S.C. App. 1987).

56. PLR 8617011. *See also* PLR 8905035, PLR 8439008, and PLR 8824014.

Further, trust remaindermen might disclaim their interests so that they can pass by intestacy to the income beneficiary, resulting in the merging of the present and future interests and the collapsing of the trust.[57] Or the life tenant and the remaindermen together might disclaim their interests, so that the trust has no beneficiaries and therefore does not exist.[58] This latter technique was used in a Connecticut case involving the will of a decedent who wanted to be sure that his ex-wife received nothing from him, even indirectly.[59] The will provided for a residuary trust to last for the life of the ex-wife. On her death, the accumulated income and principal of the trust was to be paid to their son or, if he was not then living, to the son's issue. When the father died, the son had no issue. The son filed a disclaimer. The court held that the trust could not exist without beneficiaries and directed distribution of the residuary estate to the father's intestate takers, the disclaimant and his two siblings.

J. Environmental Liability

Federal, state, and local laws each can impose liability for environmental hazards on the owner of real property on the basis of ownership alone, without regard to conduct.[60] Although exemptions are often available for fiduciaries who merely own the property, those fiduciaries may want to consider disclaiming the property so that it is clear that the fiduciary never even owned it. For example, an older article suggests a three-stage environmental audit,[61] the

57. PLR 8143144.

58. PLR 8402121. For attempted "trust busting" that did not work because of the failure of all those interested in the trust to disclaim, *see* TAMs 8851002 and 8804004.

59. *See* Paulson v. Sivaslian (Conn. Superior Ct., J. D. Litchfield 1984) (no official published opinion), printed as Appendix A to Bearns, *Connecticut Disclaimers*, 2 CONN. PROBATE L. J. 47 (1986).

60. *See* Dore, *Toxic Tort Liabilities of Real Property Owners*, 2 PROB. & PROP. NO. 1, 6 (Jan.–Feb. 1988), Shi & Moxley, *New Hazards for Fiduciaries: Environmental Liability*, 4 PROB. & PROP. NO. 6, 36 (Nov.–Dec. 1990); Vaughn, *Environmental Dangers for Fiduciaries*, 16 ACTEC NOTES 77 (1990).

61. *See* Vaughn, *supra* note 60.

results of which may suggest that not only the fiduciaries but perhaps also the beneficiaries should consider disclaiming, even to the point of allowing the property to escheat to the state if the potential liability is high enough.

K. Wrongful Death

An interesting and overlooked use of disclaimers is to change the beneficiaries of wrongful death actions. Because the amount of damages available can change depending upon the holder of the cause of action, if you change the identity of the plaintiff, you may change the size of damages.

In the *DeLuca* case,[62] a decedent who was killed by a motorist was survived by his mother and sister (with whom the decedent lived and whom the decedent supported). His sister, as personal representative, filed a wrongful death action on behalf of his mother. His mother renounced her interest in his estate, including any interest in the wrongful death recovery. The plaintiffs therefore argued that the sister alone was entitled to recover the (much higher) damages she suffered as a result of her brother's death. The defendants argued that the sister's recovery should be limited to the loss suffered by the mother, because a renunciation was a transfer of property from the mother to the daughter, and that the value of that property was the recovery in the hands of the mother.

The court, however, sided with the plaintiffs. It found that a valid renunciation is retroactive to the date of the decedent's death, and "operates as if the renouncing party had predeceased the decedent" (in other words, applying the relation-back principle). Therefore, there is no valid reason to "limit the recovery of the next distributee in line, the beneficiary of the renunciation, to the amount of pecuniary loss suffered by the renouncing party."[63] In so holding, the court overturned dicta in a previous New York

62. DeLuca v. Gallo, 287 A.D.2d 222; 735 N.Y.S.2d 596 (2001).
63. *Id.* at 228.

Supreme Court decision.[64] Because the sister was fully supported by the decedent, the damages increased significantly.

This technique does not work in all states, however; at least four (California,[65] Illinois,[66] North Carolina,[67] and Vermont[68]) have held that a disclaimer cannot be used to change the beneficiary for purposes of a wrongful death action. A fifth state court has held[69] that a daughter's disclaimer of property did not eliminate her as an heir. The court held that the fictitious deemed death rule (the relation-back principle) applied solely for purposes of determining the disposition of property and not whether the person was an heir for will purposes. If this ruling were applied to wrongful death actions, a disclaimer would be ineffective to change the "heirs" for purposes of determining who held the cause of action.

64. Larson v. Cabrini Med. Ctr., 175 Misc. 2d 573.
65. Mayo v. White, 224 Cal. Rptr. 373 (1986).
66. Boatmen's Nat'l Bank v. Direct Lines, Inc., 656 N.E.2d 1101 (Ill. 1995).
67. Evans v. Diaz, 430 S.E.2d 244 (N.C. 1993).
68. Quensel v. Town of Middlebury, 706 A.2d 436 (Vt. 1997).
69. Est. of Estes, 718 P.2d 298 (Kan. 1986).

10 DISCLAIMER PLANNING WITH GENERATION-SKIPPING TRANSFERS

Of all the aspects of estate planning, the generation-skipping transfer tax (GST Tax) can be the most frustrating. Set forth in Chapter 13 of the Code, the GST Tax imposes a tax on lifetime and testamentary transfers to persons more than one generation below the transferor at the highest marginal estate tax rate and in addition to any other transfer tax. It was designed to prevent wealthy members of an older generation from bypassing estate tax at their children's level by passing property to their grandchildren directly or through trusts. This chapter provides only a basic overview, not the nuance and complexity, of that tax.

A. Some Definitions

To understand the tax, one must first master some of the defined terms. First, a *skip person* is a person two or more generations below the transferor, or a trust if all of the trust beneficiaries are skip persons or if no person holds an interest in the trust and future distributions from the trust can be made only to skip persons.[1] A *transferor* is the person with respect to whom the transferred property was most recently subject to federal estate or gift tax (except in the case of "reverse QTIP elections under Section 2652(a)(3)).[2] The transferor is not necessarily the person who makes the transfer; if trust property is includable in a beneficiary's estate because she had a general power of appointment over that property, then upon her death she—and not the grantor of the trust—is the "transferor" for GST Tax purposes.

There are three different methods for determining generation assignments, depending upon the person's relationship to the transferor. First, a lineal descendant of a grandparent of either the transferor or the transferor's spouse is assigned to a generation measured from that common ancestor, regardless of the ages of the parties. Second, a person who at any time was married either to the transferor or to a lineal descendant of the grandparents of either the transferor or the transferor's spouse is assigned to the same generation as that spouse. Third, any person who is not described in the first two groups above is assigned to a generation relative to the transferor based upon the person's age: (1) a person born 12½ years or less after the transferor's birth is assigned to the transferor's generation; (2) a person born more than 12½ but less than 37½ years after the transferor's birth is assigned to the generation below the transferor's; and (3) an additional generation is added every 25 years.[3]

1. § 2613.
2. § 2652.
3. § 2651.

There are three different types of generation-skipping transfer:[4] a *taxable termination*[5] (the termination of an interest in property held in trust, *unless* either a non-skip person has an interest in the property immediately after the termination or at no time after the termination may a trust distribution be made to a skip person); a *direct skip*[6] (a transfer, subject to gift or estate tax, to a skip person); and a *taxable distribution*[7] (any distribution from a trust to a skip person that is not either a taxable termination or a direct skip).

Finally, there is the GST Exemption,[8] which is the amount of property that can pass free of GST Tax. This exemption can be allocated to transfers, and there are certain "automatic" allocations of exemption that are not discussed here.

B. Application of the GST Tax

The GST Tax applies differently depending upon the type of transfer made, and it can be avoided or simply does not apply in some circumstances. For example, outright lifetime transfers from a transferor to a skip person that are not subject to the gift tax (like annual exclusion gifts under Section 2503) are not subject to GST Tax. However, transfers for which no estate or gift tax liability arises because of applicable exclusion amounts under Sections 2010 or 2505 can be subject to GST Tax. The GST Tax does not apply to direct skips to which the transferor has allocated the GST Exemption or to distributions from a trust when the original transfer to that trust had GST Exemption allocated to it.

In general, transfers from *individuals* to skip persons are subject to GST Tax unless either (1) the transfer was not subject to estate or gift tax (e.g., from the annual exclusion or education/medical exceptions under Section 2503); or (2) GST Exemption is

4. § 2611.
5. § 2612(a).
6. § 2612(c).
7. § 2612(b).
8. §§ 2631 and 2632.

allocated to it. Further, transfers from a *trustee* to skip persons as to the original grantor of the trust are subject to GST Tax unless either (1) the grantor allocated GST Exemption to the full amount of the original trust transfer; (2) the trust was "grandfathered" for GST Tax purposes; or (3) the grantor is superseded as the "transferor" for GST Tax purposes.

In other words, the GST Tax can be avoided in the trust context by intentionally causing an estate tax through the use of a general power of appointment. Whether this technique is effective turns on the value of the assets in the power holder's estate; if the power holder's estate will be subject to estate tax at the top rate, then using the general power of appointment will not reduce the amount of transfer taxes paid (indeed, it may increase them in certain cases).

As discussed above, every transferor has a GST Exemption that can be allocated to transfers during life, either incrementally or to a single transfer, and that can be allocated automatically. An allocation of GST Exemption is not effective until the close of the estate tax inclusion period, or ETIP.[9] The ETIP is the period during which, if the transferor died, the transferred property would be included in the transferor's estate, and it terminates upon the first to occur of the transferor's death or the time at which no portion of the transferred property would be includable in the transferor's gross estate (except by reason of Section 2035).[10] Attempting to allocate GST Exemption during an ETIP period also is problematic because once made, the allocation of GST Exemption is irrevocable.[11] GST Exemption can be allocated to a portion, rather than all, of a trust if certain conditions are met.[12] A detailed explanation of these rules is beyond the scope of this chapter.

9. § 2642(f).

10. Treas. Reg. § 26.2632-1(c)(3).

11. For a more complete discussion of the ETIP rules, including the effect of the ETIP on split-gift transfers between spouses, *see* Treas. Reg. § 26.2632-1(c).

12. These conditions are set forth under the "separate share" rules in Treas. Reg. § 26.2654-1.

C. Grandfathered Transfers

Under grandfathering provisions, the GST Tax does not apply to a trust that was irrevocable on September 25, 1985, nor to a will executed before October 22, 1986 (date of enactment) but only if the decedent died before January 1, 1987 or was incompetent on October 22, 1986 and remained so until death.[13] Where a mother died before October 22, 1986, with a will that gave her residuary estate to her daughter or, if the daughter disclaimed, to a trust for the daughter's children, the daughter's qualified disclaimer, made after October 22, 1986, but within nine months of the mother's death, resulted in a transfer from the mother to the trust for her daughter's children to which the GST Tax does not apply.[14]

D. Using Disclaimers for GST Tax Planning

Disclaimers can be used to protect the grandfathered status of trusts. In one ruling, a will directed that the residuary estate pour into an irrevocable trust created in 1971 for the son and his family. By doing so, this residuary gift would have ended the 1971 trust's grandfathered status. The son, a beneficiary of the trust, disclaimed all of his interests in the 1971 trust with respect to the 1986 addition. The disclaimed property was to be administered as if the son had predeceased the testator and administered in a trust separate from the 1971 trust. The son's disclaimer was qualified, and "the estate and gift tax [and, presumably, also the GST Tax] provisions will apply to that interest as if it had never been transferred to the disclaimant."[15] The transfer was, instead, a transfer from a decedent who died before October 22, 1986; hence, it was a grandfathered transfer.

Disclaimers to retain the benefit of grandfathered trusts are still possible. A grandmother who died in 1989 exercised her

13. Pub. L. No. 99–514, § 1433(b).
14. PLR 8725022.
15. PLR 8705029.

testamentary nongeneral power of appointment over her deceased husband's grandfathered trust by appointing a portion of that trust to her inter vivos trust for her two grandchildren. The trust was to terminate at her death if her two grandchildren were not then living or had attained age 30, and its assets were distributable to the two grandchildren or their issue or, if none, to the grandchildren's mother. The two grandchildren, ages 22 and 19, disclaimed their interest in trust assets other than those assets that passed to the trust because of the grandmother's exercise of her power of appointment. The portion of the grandmother's trust that was funded by the exercise of the non-general power of appointment is grandfathered because her husband's will was in effect before September 25, 1985, and because the exercise of the power does not postpone or suspend vesting of any interest. The disclaiming grandchildren, the named beneficiaries of the grandmother's trust, were living when their grandfather's residuary trust was created.[16]

E. Using Disclaimers with the GST Exemption

Planning for the GST Exemption can be done by a disclaimer after the transferor's death. A surviving spouse can disclaim nonprobate property to ensure that it passes to a trust under the deceased spouse's estate plan to which exemption is to be allocated. For instance, in PLR 9038051, a husband's will provided for three $150,000 grandchildren trusts and gave his residuary estate outright to his wife, or if she failed to survive, his son and daughter-in-law, or, if they both failed to survive, to his grandchildren's trusts. The wife's partial disclaimer, backed up with disclaimers by the son and daughter-in-law, resulted in the funding of the three trusts with $333,333 apiece, instead of $150,000, thus permitting

16. PLR 9014005. *See also* PLRs 199945010 and 199945012 for other examples of the use of disclaimers by grandchildren to transfer assets of a grandfathered trust without being subject to the GST Tax.

the executor to allocate the husband's full GST Exemption to the three trusts.

Failure to fully use the decedent's GST Exemption can be cured by other disclaimers. The surviving spouse could disclaim property passing outright to him, so that the disclaimed property passed instead to a credit shelter trust. If a parent's estate passes to children and the issue of deceased children, those children who can afford to forgo all or a part of their inheritance could disclaim to permit the available GST Exemption amount to pass to their children.

F. Intentionally Disqualified Disclaimers for GST Purposes

Not all disclaimers need be qualified. Indeed, in limited circumstances (usually in the GST Tax context) having a disclaimer treated as nonqualified under Section 2518 is the planning object. In PLR 200628007, the trustee of a marital trust petitioned the court to authorize the division into marital trust A and marital trust B. These trusts were to be divided to the extent possible on a pro rata basis. The surviving spouse's three children entered into an agreement with the trustee and surviving spouse, under which they agreed to pay any resulting gift tax if the surviving spouse renounced her interest in marital trust B. As a result of the surviving spouse's disclaimer, which would not be qualified under Section 2518, the sons' remainder interests in marital trust B would accelerate, they each would receive a third of the trust property, and they would be responsible for the payment of gift taxes as a result of the nonqualified disclaimer. The Internal Revenue Service (IRS) ruled that the division of the trusts did not affect the "marital deduction" status of the trusts, that the disclaimer was not qualified under Section 2518 and therefore a tax liability resulted, that the sons were responsible for paying that tax liability, and that there were no adverse tax consequences to marital trust A or to another trust that was part of the decedent's estate plan. In other words, parts of a qualified terminable interest property (QTIP) trust were used to fund a net gift from the surviving spouse to her children.

In PLR 200530002, a taxpayer proposed to renounce, many years after it was created, a one-fifth remainder interest in a trust created before January 1, 1977, while retaining the right to income over the entire trust. Because Section 2702 applied, the disclaimant's retained income interest in the trust was valued at zero, so the value of his taxable transfer was equal to one-fifth of the total value of the trust property. Because the disclaimant became the "transferor" for generation-skipping transfer tax purposes, the trust property became subject to Chapter 13.

Finally, PLR 200901013 held that nonqualified disclaimers of trust interests by children of the settlors resulted in the children becoming "transferors" for GST Tax purposes. As a result, a taxable termination occurred at the time of the disclaimer, but only as to the interests held by the settlors' grandchildren at the time of the disclaimer. Regarding the portions of the trust over which the disclaimants were treated as transferors, neither the trust nor any of the settlors' grandchildren were subject to GST Tax on future distributions.

G. Other Uses for Disclaimers

The following are some additional uses of disclaimers for postmortem GST Tax planning:[17]

- Disclaimers can be used to intentionally create direct skips rather than taxable terminations (for example, if property passes in trust for the benefit of both children and grandchildren, the children would disclaim their interests in the property to convert what would otherwise be a taxable termination into a direct skip). Because the tax on direct skips is tax exclusive rather than tax inclusive, the GST Tax is reduced. However, it is also due earlier, at the death of the transferor rather than the death of the child.
- Disclaimers can limit transfers to the amount of the available GST Exemption. Skip persons can disclaim their

17. *Id.*

interests in overfunded trusts if, under state law or the instrument, the property would pass to non-skip persons. This could be done through a formula geared to preservation of the GST Exemption.

- Disclaimers can help ensure proper funding with hard-to-value assets. Transferring business interests, for instance, can be difficult when those transfers should be no more than the current amount of GST Exemption, because such interests are difficult to value. One solution might be to place such assets in a lifetime QTIP trust for the spouse and, then, within nine months and without the spouse accepting any benefits, have the spouse disclaim, through a formula provision, such amounts of property as are necessary to take full advantage of the transferor spouse's GST Exemption.

Disclaimers can take advantage of the predeceased parent exemption. If a transferor dies leaving a surviving spouse, a child and children of a predeceased child, and if the surviving spouse, through a power of appointment, for example, has the power to vary dispositions between families, a disclaimer by the surviving child and his or her descendants should be considered. Disclaimers by the living child and all of his or her living descendants (if any) that result in property passing directly from the transferor to the predeceased child's descendants would qualify for the predeceased parent exemption under Section 2651(d). The surviving spouse could then, through some other means, provide greater benefits for the disclaimants.

DISCLAIMERS FOR INCOME TAX PLANNING

11

Disclaimers are not typically thought of in the income tax context, and their primary use is in connection with transfer taxes. However, there are income tax benefits to be gained without transfer tax cost by using disclaimers.

A. Generally

Section 2518 applies only to transfer, not income, taxes[1] and, in at least one instance, the Internal Revenue Service (IRS) has refused to rule on the income

1. There is at least one income tax reference to disclaimers. Section 678(a) deems a person other than the grantor of a trust to be the owner of the trust if that person can appoint the corpus or income to himself, with the result that, under § 671, that trust's income is taxable to that person. However, § 678(d) declares that § 678(a) "shall not apply with respect to a power which has been renounced or disclaimed within a reasonable time after the holder of the power first became aware of its existence."

tax consequences of a qualified disclaimer.[2] However, disclaimers do create income tax consequences and planning opportunities. In the independent retirement account (IRA) context, for instance, a surviving wife's disclaimer of her interest in her deceased husband's rollover IRA allowed a trust for the benefit of a disabled child to become the payee.[3] Additional examples of IRA income tax planning are described in Chapter 9.

In dictum contained in an income tax refund case,[4] the district court stated that it was "of the opinion that the same principles apply to an income tax deduction as well as to an estate."[5] Further, the IRS has occasionally ruled on the income tax consequences of disclaimers. One now-outdated private letter ruling[6] addressed the impact of a disclaimer on the income tax consequences of a family contributing real property that generated oil and gas royalties to a new partnership. By disclaiming an interest in those properties, the mother allowed the disclaimed property interest to pass to her children as heirs, not transferees, which in turn avoided a disallowance of percentage depletion under Section 613A(c)(9) (as it existed then). In another ruling,[7] a surviving spouse disclaimed her trust income interest in property left to a testamentary trust that was sold during the estate administration. The property was treated as if it passed directly to the children at the decedent's death, allowing them to make a Section 1033(a)(2) election not to recognize gain realized upon the sale of the property.

B. Tax-Favored Corporate Redemptions

Section 303 treats a stock redemption in a decedent's estate as a sale rather than a dividend distribution to the extent that the proceeds do not exceed the death taxes and deductible funeral and

2. PLR 8039018.
3. PLR 9037048.
4. Simmons v. U.S., 80-1 U.S.T.C. Para. 9,287 (D. Ariz. 1980).
5. 80-1 U.S.T.C. at para. 83,614.
6. PLR 8741073.
7. TAM 9232004.

administration expenses of the estate. In PLR 8149050, a wife left all of her shares of stock in a closely held corporation to a trust that gave her husband the discretionary right to income and the right to vote the stock. The remainder beneficiaries of the trust were the couple's adult children, and the residuary beneficiaries of the wife's estate were her grandchildren. Because the estate residue was inadequate to pay anything to the grandchildren after paying death taxes and funeral and administration expenses, all trust beneficiaries disclaimed their interests in enough shares of stock needed to pay those expenses, allowing the estate to take advantage of Section 303. Note that, if the estate's basis for the shares was close to the redemption price, the residuary gift to the grandchildren would have generated little if any income or transfer tax cost.

Disclaimers frequently are used to facilitate a Section 302 stock redemption, whether it be a "substantially disproportionate" redemption[8] or a "complete termination of interest" redemption.[9] If the redemption qualifies under Section 302, it is treated as a sale rather than as a dividend distribution. Typically in these rulings, either the parent from whom stock will be redeemed disclaims all of her interest in a trust that holds stock in the redeeming corporation, or the principal shareholder disclaims his or her interest in the trust that holds the stock to be redeemed. Because the transfer tax cost of these transactions is rarely important, these Section 302 ruling requests do not usually ask for a ruling that the disclaimers are qualified.

C. S Corporations

Trusts can be S corporation shareholders, but only if the trust is a qualified subchapter S trust (QSST)[10] or an electing small business trust (ESBT). A QSST must have only one income beneficiary to

8. PLR 8117202.

9. PLR 9041005, PLR 9014015, PLR 8610039, PLR 8546117, PLR 8542066, PLR 8406051, and PLR 8107073.

10. § 1361(c), (d).

whom all of the trust income is or must be currently distributed; it must terminate on the death of that income beneficiary or sooner; and it may distribute corpus during the term of the trust or at its termination only to that beneficiary. If other permissible beneficiaries disclaim their interests in the trust, such disclaimers may allow the trust to qualify for QSST treatment.[11]

D. Basis

If a person receives a gift of low-basis property shortly before the donor's death, and the donee would have received the property anyway at the donor's death, the donee can disclaim the gift in order to obtain the date of death, rather than the carryover, basis.[12] The property will be included in the donor's estate, and the basis for the distributee will be the estate tax value.[13]

Gifts of appreciated property made to a decedent are denied a basis step-up under Section 1014(e) if the gift's fair market value exceeds the donor's adjusted basis; if the gift was made within the one-year period ending on the date of the decedent's death; and if the property was acquired from the decedent by, or passed directly or indirectly from the decedent to, the donor or the donor's spouse.[14] If this rule applies, that property it applies to retains the donor's basis.

This rule can be avoided if the donee lives for more than a year after the date of the gift or if the acquirer from the donee's estate is not the donor. If the donor gives the appreciated property outright to the donee and the donee dies intestate within one year, a disclaimer can be used within nine months after the death of the donee to ensure that the appreciated property does not pass from the deceased donee to the donor (or the spouse of the donor).

---

11. *See, e.g.*, PLR 8825055 (although the disclaimers were not qualified because they were executed long after the deaths, in 1979 and 1981, of the two testators whose wills established the trusts, the cleansing disclaimers qualified the trusts as QSSTs under § 1361(d)(3)).

12. *See* PLR 9043050 and PLR 8723033.

13. § 2518(b)(3), Regs. § 25.2518-2(d). *See also* PLR 9043050.

14. § 1014(e).

Avoiding application of Section 1014(e) may have been the reason behind a disclaimer by a husband who gave stock to his wife before she died.[15] The husband disclaimed all his interests in the trust his wife created and funded with the stock that she had received from her husband and that was includible in her gross estate. The trust property, therefore, passed to the children and took the wife's date-of-death value as its basis.

15. PLR 8628030.

12 DISCLAIMER PLANNING FOR CREDITOR AVOIDANCE

The overwhelming use for disclaimers is in the area of federal gift tax avoidance. If there were no federal gift tax, beneficiaries would simply accept the property and then transfer it to the people they want to receive it. A disclaimer is rarely used for non-tax, state law purposes.

When such disclaimers do occur, they are almost always centered on some form of creditor avoidance. Such avoidance was the reason renunciations (or disclaimers) were invented in England several centuries ago, and is still a significant motive for disclaimers today. The creditors to be avoided may include the federal government (in the form of tax liens), bankruptcy trustees, or state benefits administrators. As the following discussion shows, some of those creditors can be avoided, while others cannot.

A. Federal Law of Tax Liens

Sorry, but the federal government will get its money, regardless of disclaimers. The United States Supreme Court has ruled[1] that, in the context of federal tax liens, a debtor's disclaimer of property cannot defeat the ability of the Internal Revenue Service (IRS) to attach the disclaimed property. In that case, an insolvent debtor, at the time of his mother's death, owed $325,000 in unpaid tax assessments. The IRS had valid tax liens against all of his "property and rights to property" under Section 6321. The debtor disclaimed his distribution from his mother's estate, so that it passed instead to his daughter. She, in turn, transferred the property to a spendthrift trust for the benefit of the debtor (her father) and his spouse. The U.S. Supreme Court held that federal, not state, law governs property rights under Section 6321. While state law defines a taxpayer's property rights that the government initially seeks to levy, federal law determines whether those state law rights qualify as property interests for purposes of federal tax liens. The Court also ruled that, under Arkansas law, the debtor had a valuable and transferable right to his mother's estate that could not be written off as a more personal right to accept or reject property, virtually ignoring the relation-back doctrine.

A U.S. District Court in Tennessee[2] applied the *Drye* decision to a slightly different set of facts. There, the personal representative of the decedent's estate sought determination of funds held in escrow; the potential distributees were the decedent's son, the decedent's widow, and the IRS. At the time of the decedent's death, son had several federal tax liens outstanding against him. The decedent died holding an annuity naming son as the primary and widow as the contingent beneficiary. Eight months after the decedent's death, son disclaimed his interest in the annuity proceeds. Relying on *Drye*, the IRS argued that the liens attached to the entire value of the annuity at the time of the decedent's death and were not defeated by the disclaimer. Son argued that a close reading of

1. Drye v. U.S., 528 U.S. 49, 120 S. Ct. 474 (1999).
2. Choate v. Tubbs, 2003-1 U.S.T.C. Para. 50, 402; 91 A.F.T.R.2d 1881.

Drye showed that the opposite result was appropriate, because the Supreme Court relied on the "crucial distinction" between disclaimers of lifetime gifts versus those of a bequest or inheritance. Son argued that the disclaimer of the annuity proceeds "paved the way for his father's wishes, as evidenced by the terms of his Last Will and Testament to be carried out." Widow argued that the disclaimer was made solely to enter into a family agreement to carry out the decedent's wishes. The court found neither the son's nor the widow's arguments persuasive; son's motives had no bearing on the question of whether he possessed a property right subject to the tax liens; and once the decedent died, the status quo could not be restored. As a result, the court ruled in favor of the IRS, holding that the annuity proceeds were subject to the tax liens.

Finally, a Florida district court decision[3] held that the *Drye* decision applies only to inheritances that are disclaimed after the federal tax lien attaches. In this case, a tax lien was not filed until two years after a husband disclaimed a one-half interest in a home left to him under his wife's will, with the result that the interest passed to the couple's children rather than being available to satisfy a tax lien.

B. Federal Bankruptcy Law

Federal bankruptcy law has its own law of fraudulent transfer that focuses on whether the disclaimer was a voidable "transfer." Three decisions decided before *Drye* found that disclaimers were not "transfers" under the Bankruptcy Code. First, the Seventh Circuit in *Atchison*[4] ruled that a debtor who disclaimed her interest in her deceased father's estate three months before she filed bankruptcy never possessed the property under Illinois law as a result of the relation-back doctrine. Therefore, she could not have made a fraudulent conveyance.

3. U.S. v. Weisman,102 A.F.T.R.2d 2008-6874.

4. *In re* Atchison, 925 F.2d 209 (7th Cir. 1991) *cert. denied sub nom.*, Jones v. Atchison, 112 S. Ct. 178 (1991) (discussed below).

Second, the Fifth Circuit[5] held that a debtor's disclaimer of his deceased father's property was valid even though the debtor filed a bankruptcy petition the next day. The court also held that, due to the relation-back doctrine, a valid disclaimer cannot be a fraudulent transfer under the Bankruptcy Code, because the debtor is deemed never to have possessed the property. The court relied on the *Atchison* decision, specifically rejecting the Bankruptcy Court's holding.[6]

Finally, the Tenth Circuit, in a Pre-Bankruptcy Code decision, held that, under Colorado's disclaimer law, the disclaimed property of a decedent passed as though the disclaimant had predeceased the decedent. Therefore, a timely disclaimer of property under Colorado law could not be a transfer for bankruptcy law purposes. Although not referring to it directly, the court essentially adopted the relation-back doctrine.

Although three Bankruptcy Court decisions held that a disclaimer is a "transfer" for bankruptcy law purposes, two[7] were decided in the Southern District of Texas (appealable to the Fifth Circuit) before *Simpson*, which rejected their rationale, while the third,[8] a Pre-Bankruptcy Code case, was rejected by the Seventh Circuit in *Atchison*. Therefore, before 1999, it seemed relatively clear that a pre-petition disclaimer was effective in keeping disclaimed property out of the bankruptcy estate by applying the relation-back doctrine.

However, given that the U.S. Supreme Court in *Drye* held that the state law property doctrine of relation back was ineffective in the context of federal tax liens, it raised the question whether bankruptcy courts would follow suit and find that federal bankruptcy rules also trumped state law property rights. Although courts have gone both ways on this question, the weight of authority is that the logic in *Drye* does not apply to bankruptcy law.

---

5. Simpson v. Penner, 36 F.3d 450 (5th Cir. 1994).
6. *In re* Brajkovic, 151 B.R. 402 (Bank. W.D. Tex. 1993).
7. *Id.*; *also* Casciato v. Stevens, 112 B.R. 175 (Bkrtcy. S.D. Tex. 1989).
8. *In re* Peery, 40 B.R. 811 (Bkrtcy. M.D. Tenn. 1984).

The Ninth Circuit has taken up this issue twice. In the first case,[9] it held that a disclaimer of an inheritance from the debtor's father made five months before the debtor filed a bankruptcy petition was not a transfer, and therefore the disclaimed property was not available to creditors. The lower court held that Washington's disclaimer law had a relation-back feature, preventing the disclaimant from ever having acquired an interest in the disclaimed property. The Ninth Circuit Bankruptcy panel, hearing the matter de novo, agreed, relying on *Simpson* and *Atchison* rather than *Brajkovic* and *Peery*. The problem with this decision, however, is that it was decided so shortly after *Drye* that it is unclear whether the parties or the court considered that decision. Indeed, the opinion does not even refer to that case.

However, the second case[10] addresses the question directly, and with the same result. In this case, the debtor was a beneficiary of her father's revocable trust upon his death. Eight months after his death, the debtor disclaimed her claims to the trust property; and less than a month after that, she filed a petition in bankruptcy court. The bankruptcy trustee sought to avoid the disclaimer, arguing that the *Bright* decision was undermined by *Drye*. The trustee asked the Ninth Circuit to extend the *Drye* rationale to the bankruptcy context. The court declined to do so, however, for several reasons. First, the timing in *Drye* was different; there, the tax lien was already in place, whereas the debtor in this case disclaimed before filing the bankruptcy petition. Second, *Drye* was a tax lien case, which was legally distinguishable from the bankruptcy context, which "largely respects substantive state law rights." As a result, the court refused to extend *Drye* to bankruptcy cases and ruled that the disclaimer was not a transfer.

In a Fifth Circuit case,[11] the owner of a tanning-booth company sued one of its customers for defamation and trade disparagement but lost, with the result that the customer was entitled to attorneys' fees of almost $400,000. The owner was unable to pay. On the same day the judgment was entered, the owner's father died

9. *In re* Bright, 241 B.R. 664 (9th Cir. 1999).
10. *In re* Costas, 555 F.3d 790 (2009).
11. Laughlin v. Nouveau Body and Tan, LLC, 602 F.3d 417 (5th Cir. 2010).

in Louisiana. As a result, the owner was entitled to a quarter of his father's estate under intestacy. Four months later, the owner renounced any interest in his father's estate, allowing the property to pass to his daughter, who ultimately gave the funds to her grandmother (the decedent's wife). Six weeks after renouncing the interest in the estate, the owner filed a Chapter 7 bankruptcy petition. The creditor (the owner's former customer) argued, and the bankruptcy court agreed, that under the *Drye* holding the renunciation was a fraudulent transfer.

The Fifth Circuit, however, overturned the bankruptcy court's decision. Relying on both *Costas* and *Simpson* (and distinguishing *Drye*), the court found that although the bankruptcy code defines *transfer*, state law defines *property* and *interest in property* absent a controlling federal interest. The *Drye* case was distinguishable from these facts because it involved the "particularities and structure" of the Internal Revenue Code, and because in the case at hand (as in the *Costas* case) the renunciation was made prepetition, whereas in *Drye* the disclaimer was made post–tax lien. Therefore, *Simpson* is still good law, and Louisiana law had to be applied to determine whether "property" was transferred.[12] The court held that "a valid pre-petition renunciation of an inheritance interest is not a transfer of the debtor's property" for bankruptcy purposes.[13]

Other courts have followed the same logic. First, an Oklahoma bankruptcy decision[14] held specifically that *Drye* does not apply to bankruptcy pre-petition disclaimers. The facts were very similar to those in the other cases: The disclaimant was insolvent when she executed the disclaimer, her interest in the disclaimed property had vested before the disclaimer was executed, and she filed the Chapter 7 petition *the day after* she filed the disclaimer. The bankruptcy trustee argued, under *Drye*, that the disclaimer was a fraudulent conveyance under the Bankruptcy Code. The court disagreed with this logic for the same reasons as those in *Costas*: the disclaimant in *Drye* executed his disclaimer after the tax lien

12. *Id.* at 426.
13. *Id.* at 428.
14. *In re* Falk, 281 B.R. 15 (West. Dist. Okla. 2002).

had attached, which would be the equivalent of a *post-petition* disclaimer in the bankruptcy context, and the Supreme Court's decision was based on the specific language of Section 6321, and the Court referred only to tax lien cases in support of its holding. As a result, the court held that

> [r]egardless of the unfortunate effect on creditors, if the state disclaimer law is to be followed, as the U.S. Supreme Court and Circuit Courts have required, it is axiomatic that the debtor's timely filed disclaimer had the effect of preventing the debtor from owning an interest in the disclaimed property. Without an interest in property there was nothing to transfer. And without a transfer there was not a fraudulent transfer under Section 548(a) of the Bankruptcy Code.[15]

The bankruptcy court granted summary judgment in favor of the disclaimant and against the bankruptcy trustee.

Other bankruptcy courts have reached similar conclusions. An Oregon decision applying North Dakota law[16] found that the North Dakota disclaimer statute provided that disclaimers related back for all purposes, including keeping disclaimed assets out of the bankruptcy estate, and that *Drye* applied only to federal tax liens, not bankruptcy proceedings. A North Carolina decision,[17] dealing with the question of whether tenancy by the entireties property should be includable in the bankruptcy estate, also concluded that *Drye* did not apply when determining bankruptcy property rights. Finally, an Eighth Circuit decision,[18] decided after *Drye*, held that a pre-petition disclaimer was not a fraudulent conveyance under Missouri law. However, the court stated that it was not facing the question "whether *Drye* carries over to the federal bankruptcy fraud context," and it saved "that issue for another day."[19]

15. *Id.* at 21.
16. *In re* Nistler, 259 B.R. 723 (2001).
17. *In re* Knapp, 285 B.R. 176 (2002).
18. *In re* Popkin & Stern, 223 F.3d 764 (8th Cir. 2000).
19. *Id.* at 769.

One bankruptcy decision[20] held that *Drye* applied in the federal bankruptcy context, so that disclaimed assets are pulled into the bankruptcy estate. Here, a debtor disclaimed a real property interest the day before he filed a bankruptcy petition. In ruling in favor of the bankruptcy trustee, the court observed that "[s]ubstantial authority holds that the disclaimer of an inheritance is not a transfer which can form the basis of a fraudulent transfer,"[21] including the *Simpson*, *Atchison*, and *Bright* cases. However, the bankruptcy court ignored these decisions, instead applying the *Drye* rationale. It held that the "artificially created" state doctrine of relation back cannot override federal law and that the Supreme Court's opinion "broadly suggests that, in all contexts, the result would be the same."[22]

Nevertheless, this one case stands against the clear weight of the case law, including cases decided by the Fifth, Eighth, and Ninth Circuits. Given that *Kloubec* ignored the significant authority holding that pre-petition disclaimers are not transfers for bankruptcy purposes, and given that the weight of post-*Drye* decisions appears to support that authority, it seems clear that *Kloubec* was wrongly decided. However, it also seems clear that bankruptcy courts are still listening to the argument that the *Drye* rationale could be extended to the pre-petition disclaimers.

C. State Law of Fraudulent Conveyance

Many states have adopted the Uniform Fraudulent Transfer Act (UFTA), under which a creditor of an insolvent debtor may avoid certain transfers, including those made without receiving a reasonably equivalent value in exchange. Does this mean that disclaimers are "transfers" that can be avoided? Several states have enacted legislation preventing an insolvent debtor from disclaim-

20. *In re* Kloubec, 247 B.R. 246 (2000).
21. *Id.* at 254.
22. *Id.* at 256.

ing.[23] For those states that have not done so, cases from different states come down on different sides. The majority view, however, is that the relation-back doctrine means that a disclaimer cannot be a fraudulent transfer because it is not a "transfer." Further, the Comments to the Uniform Disclaimer of Transfers Under Nontestamentary Instruments Act support this position, stating that, with regard to creditors, "the provision for 'relation back' has the legal effect of preventing a succession from becoming operative in favor of the disclaimant. The relation back is 'for all purposes' which would include, among others, for the purpose of rights of creditors."[24]

This was the view of a Texas court of appeals.[25] The court held that Texas adopted the relation-back doctrine, under which the disclaimant is treated as predeceasing the transfer of the disclaimed property, which "prevents a disclaimer from being treated as a transfer under fraudulent transfer acts, absent an express statutory provision to the contrary." The Supreme Court of Nebraska[26] reached the same conclusion. In that case, fifteen months after the creditors of a disclaimant obtained a judgment against him, his mother died, naming him as one of her beneficiaries. Two months after her death, the creditors sought to satisfy their judgment from the proceeds of the estate; and two months after that, the disclaimant renounced his interest in the estate. The supreme court held that a renunciation is not a "transfer" and therefore cannot be a "fraudulent transfer." The court observed that

> it is the majority view that a renunciation under the applicable state probate code is not treated as a fraudulent transfer of assets under the UFTA, and creditors of the person making a renunciation cannot claim any rights

23. *See, e.g.*, FLA. STAT. ANN. § 732.801(6) (2004); MASS. GEN. LAWS ANN. ch. 191A § 8 (2003); MINN. STAT. ANN. § 525.532(c)(6) (2003).

24. The comments quoted here are from the Uniform Disclaimer of Transfers by Will, Intestacy or Appointment Act; however, the comments specifically refer to and adopt the comments to the Uniform Disclaimer of Transfer Under Nontestamentary Instruments Act.

25. Dyer v. Eckols, 808 S.W. 2d 531 (Tex. App. 1991).

26. Essen v. Gilmore, 259 Neb. 55; 607 N.W.2d 829 (2000).

> to the renounced property in the absence of an express statutory provision to the contrary.[27]

The court further noted that, while several states enacted legislation preventing a debtor from disclaiming benefits under a will, thus enhancing the creditor's rights, Nebraska was not such a state.

The District Court for South Carolina, in an unreported decision,[28] reached a similar conclusion. In this case, a debtor disclaimed his interest in his mother's estate the day before he was sued for sexual harassment and intentional infliction of emotional distress. When asked at trial why he disclaimed, the debtor said that he wanted to benefit his brother's children from the inheritance because he had none of his own, and that he did not know when he executed the disclaimer that the civil suit was about to be filed. The court, in upholding the validity of the disclaimer, also noted that it is "the majority view that a creditor cannot prevent a debtor from disclaiming an inheritance." Further, the few states supporting the minority view that a disclaimer can constitute a fraudulent conveyance follow a California decision[29] that itself was overturned by the California legislature. Finally, decisions from Indiana,[30] Virginia,[31] Michigan,[32] and North Dakota[33] all have found that disclaimers were not fraudulent conveyances.

On the other hand, several cases hold that disclaimers are void when the disclaimant does so with the actual intent to defraud a creditor. For instance, the Ohio Supreme Court[34] addressed a situation in which a disclaimant hit and killed a pedestrian while driving under the influence. On the same day the pedestrian died, the disclaimant sold his wife his interest in their home for a dol-

---

27. *Id.* at 61–62.
28. Pauw v. Agee, 2000 U.S. Dist. LEXIS 22323.
29. *In re* Kalt's Estate, 16 Cal. 2d 807; 108 P.2d 401 (1940).
30. Frances Slocum Bank & Trust Co. v. Est. of Martin, 666 N.E.2d 411 (Ind. App. 1996).
31. Abbott v. Willey, 253 Va. 88, 479 S.E.2d 528 (1997).
32. Baltrusaitis v. Cook, 174 Mich. App. 180; 435 N.W.2d 417 (Mich. Ct. App. 1988).
33. *In re* Estate of Opatz, 554 N.W.2d 813 (N.D. 1996).
34. Stein v. Brown, 18 Ohio St. 3d 305; 480 N.E.2d 1121 (1985).

lar. Eight months later, the disclaimant's brother died, leaving half his estate to the disclaimant; and three months after his brother's death (and after a wrongful death action had been filed against the disclaimant by the victim's mother), the disclaimant renounced his interest in his brother's estate. The court, ruling in favor of the victim's mother, first noted that an increasing number of states have ruled that a renunciation is a transfer, and when it is done to defraud a creditor, it can be attacked. The disclaimant's transfer of his residence to his spouse for a dollar on the same day that the victim died was "prima facie fraudulent,"[35] and the disclaimer was merely a further attempt to divest future assets. When it viewed "the totality of the circumstances," the court could not condone such action, holding that "where a will beneficiary seeks to disclaim an inheritance pursuant to [the Ohio disclaimer statute] with the actual intent to defraud a present or future creditor," the disclaimer is a fraudulent conveyance and can be set aside.[36]

Relying on this case, the Bankruptcy Court for the Northern District of Ohio reached the same conclusion. Here, a partner in a law firm that faced liability had filed for Chapter 11 protection. He later converted it to a Chapter 7 proceeding, and about the same time disclaimed his interest in his mother's estate. Although he did not deny that one reason for the disclaimer was to avoid creditors, he also claimed he had estate planning reasons for doing so (even though he never stated exactly what they were). The court found that he intended to defraud creditors and that the estate planning argument was mere pretext, so it barred the disclaimer.

D. Medicaid Qualification

Disclaimers also can be used in some limited situations to ensure that the disclaimant qualifies (or continues to qualify) for Medicare benefits by avoiding receipt of assets that might disqualify the disclaimant. However, this approach does not work in all states. Some have adopted legislation specifically preventing

35. *Id.* at 309.
36. *Id.*

such a disclaimer.[37] Those states without such legislation may still prevent such disclaimers under their general statutes preventing fraudulent conveyances.

For those states without general or specific statutory prohibitions, the trend in court decisions is toward preventing disclaimers done to keep the disclaimant qualified for state or federal benefits. In one of the first cases, decided in Connecticut,[38] the sister of the decedent (and a one-third beneficiary of the decedent's estate) had received federal benefits for eleven years before the decedent's death. The sister tried to disclaim her interest in the decedent's estate, but the statute allowing state participation in the federal benefits program prohibited disposition of assets by an aid recipient without permission from state authorities. The court found that this statute barred the relation-back provision of the disclaimer statute. Therefore, the disclaimer was invalid and the sister's eligibility for aid could be reevaluated by the state.[39]

The New York Supreme Court[40] also agreed with the state's determination that a disclaimant's renunciation of an inheritance caused her Medicaid benefits to be discontinued. Regardless of the disclaimant's absolute right to refuse to accept a gift, her failure to pursue an available resource, in violation of the state Medicaid statute, resulted in disqualification.[41] North Dakota,[42] Maryland,[43] and Wisconsin[44] courts also have ruled that a disclaimer of an

37. *See, e.g.*, Or. Rev. Stat. § 105.648 (2003), which bars a disclaimer when the disclaimant is indebted to the state for fraudulently obtained public assistance. Such legislation may be part of a growing trend. *See* LaPiana, *Some Property Law Issues in the Law of Disclaimers*, 38 Real Prop., Prob. & Trust J. 207, 234 (2003).

38. State v. Murtha, 427 A.2d 807 (Conn. 1980).

39. This decision was followed in several subsequent Connecticut cases. *See, e.g.*, Dep't of Income Maint. v. Watts, 558 A.2d 998 (Conn. 1989).

40. *In re Molloy*, 214 A.D.2d 171; 631 N.Y.S.2d 910 (1995).

41. *See also* In the Matter of Keuning v. Perales, 190 A.D.2d 1033; 593N.Y.S.2d 653 (1993).

42. Hinschberger v. Griggs, 499 N.W.2d 876 (N.D. 1993).

43. Troy v. Hart, 116 Md. App. 468; 697 A.2d 113 (1997).

44. Tannler v. Wis. Dep't of Health & Soc. Serv., 211 Wis. 2d 179; 564 N.W.2d 735 (1997).

inheritance by a public benefits recipient results in that disclaimant being disqualified from receiving such benefits.

On the other hand, at least one state court[45] ruled that a disclaimer does not disqualify the disclaimant from receiving benefits. There, the court found that the Iowa disclaimer law could frustrate the collection of Medicare claims. However, Iowa courts repeatedly acknowledged that beneficiaries can renounce property even if such renunciation frustrates the claims of creditors. Because the Iowa disclaimer law does not result in a transfer of property, there could be no "scheme" to circumvent the Medicaid eligibility provisions. Nevertheless, the weight of authority in this area is that disclaimers result in a disqualification of federal and state Medicaid benefits. Indeed, even the Medicare Assistance Handbook defines a *transfer* to include the "waiver of an inheritance."[46]

This line of cases raises the question about this distinction between Medicaid benefits and fraudulent conveyances. It seems contradictory that the same authority holding that disclaimers are not fraudulent conveyances also holds that disclaimers are disqualifying transfers for Medicaid purposes. The two can be distinguished, to some extent, by the fact that state Medicaid statutes have specific rules regarding disqualifying transfers, and therefore the Medicaid line of cases is limited only to those situations.

45. *In re Kirk*, 591 N.W.2d 630 (Iowa 1999).
46. *Id.* (citing 42 U.S.C.A. § 1396p(e)(1) (2000)).

POTENTIAL DISCLAIMER PROBLEMS 13

As already noted, many requirements must be met, and a great deal of thought has to be given, to a proper disclaimer. This chapter provides a list of issues that need to be thought through fully to ensure that disclaimer planning is done correctly.

A. Drafting for Disclaimers

Disclaimers are not useful only to fix defective plans; they can also be incorporated into estate plans. As prior chapters on credit shelter drafting, planning for qualified plans, and IRAs and GST planning have shown, disclaimers incorporated into an estate plan provide flexibility for unanticipated future events and for changes in tax law, the economic position of the testator, or the relative situations of beneficiaries.

In an earlier example conceived before the unlimited marital deduction, husband created five trusts: Trust A, Trust B, the Non-Marital Trust, the Family Trust, and the 1981 Trust. The trusts were created for the benefit of the wife, with the exception of the 1981 Trust, which was created for the grandchildren. Upon disclaimers by the wife, Trust A passed to the Non-Marital Trust; Trust B and the Non-Marital Trust passed to the Family Trust; and the Family Trust would pass to the 1981 Trust. Upon the husband's death and after several disclaimers by the wife, Trusts A and B and the Non-Marital Trust all ended up in the Family Trust.[1]

Other examples include documents that provide for specific gifts of real estate to pass to charity if disclaimed by children;[2] for disclaimed property of child A to pass outright to his children, but disclaimed property of child B to pass into trust for hers;[3] and for residue disclaimed by a child to pass to trusts for the son's four children.[4] In each of these cases, the disclaimer planning was implemented when the estate planning documents were drafted.

Disclaimer drafting can be very complicated. In PLR 200442027, husband's revocable living trust provided that if the wife took no action, trust assets were to be distributed to a nine-month-long trust for her benefit, paying her all the trust income and distributable to her on termination; if she disclaimed her interest in this initial trust, the disclaimed assets passed to a second trust; if she disclaimed any interest in this second trust, it passed to a third; and so on. As a result of these "cascading disclaimers," up to five trusts could be created. The first three trusts were drafted to qualify for qualified terminable interest property (QTIP) treatment, while the fourth and fifth were pot trusts for the benefit of the wife and issue. The wife proposed disclaiming her entire interest in the initial trust; a portion of her interest in the second trust that passed as a result of her first disclaimer; and so on until all five trusts held some portion of her husband's assets (the dollar amounts of each disclaimer were not disclosed). The Internal Revenue Service (IRS) ruled that each disclaimer would be qualified and the property passing to each of the four trusts would be

1. PLR 8749013, PLR 8726030, and PLR 8638011.
2. *See, e.g.*, PLR 8626046, PLR 9113004.
3. PLR 8821017.
4. PLR 8509092.

treated as though it passed directly from the husband's revocable trust.

At least one commentator has speculated about the purpose of this estate,[5] identifying several possible planning issues to be addressed (none of which was very satisfactory): reciprocal trust doctrine concerns, under- or overperformance hedge on the gift, or the basis for a "formula" disclaimer. The point, however, is that disclaimer planning can be fine-tuned to create many different possible results.

B. What Happens to Disclaimed Property—Determining the Identity of the Beneficiary

The most important step in avoiding disclaimer problems seems to be the most obvious: specifying who gets the disclaimed property. State law governs the way in which disclaimed interests pass. As already mentioned, the paradigmatic rule is that disclaimed property passes as if the disclaimant were not alive to take the disclaimed property at the time of the transfer. Although this "deemed death" rule is easy to apply in the case of present interests, it can become more complex. For outright will gifts, the disclaimant must first look to relevant provisions of the will (which might state where property passes if the disclaimant predeceases the testator). However, if there are no such provisions, then the testamentary gift lapses and anti-lapse statutes (of which almost every jurisdiction has some version) may come into play. These typically provide that, if a beneficiary who predeceases a testator is related to that testator, the gift then passes to the beneficiary's issue. The scope of a state's anti-lapse statute can vary; one state might provide that the anti-lapse statute applies to gifts to descendants of the grandparents of the testator.[6]

5. *"Cascading" Disclaimers Were Found to Be Qualified Disclaimers—But What Was the Taxpayer Doing?* J. of Tax'n (Dec. 2004).

6. *See, e.g.*, Uniform Prob. Code § 2-603(b)(3).

Non-probate transfers may be more complicated because few jurisdictions have anti-lapse statutes that apply to such transfers. If the property passes under a revocable trust, the trust terms will govern; but if the trust is silent, then the disclaimed property will pass with the trust residue to the decedent's estate (and perhaps through intestacy). For property that passes by beneficiary designation (like life insurance and retirement benefits), a beneficiary's disclaimed property may pass to a contingent beneficiary if one is named. If not, either the insurance company or retirement plan will dictate where the property passes, or it will pass to the insured's or plan participant's estate. In other words, the disposition of non-probate assets after a disclaimer may not be clear.

1. Passage of Future Interests

Even worse is the passage following disclaimer of a future interest. For example, if the disclaimant is the remainder beneficiary of a testamentary trust and disclaims that future interest during the income beneficiary's lifetime, the disclaimed property typically passes as though the disclaimant predeceased the testator. However, what happens if, after the disclaimer but before the death of the income beneficiary, the disclaimant has another child? The disclaimant's children living at the time of the testator's death could argue that this after-born child is not entitled to trust property because, had the disclaimant truly predeceased the testator, the after-born child would not exist. Some statutes, including the 1999 Disclaimer Act, avoid the problem by having the deemed death of the disclaimant occur immediately before the time of distribution of the interest, which is defined as the time "when a disclaimed interest would have taken effect in possession or enjoyment."[7]

This potential flaw in some states' disclaimer statutes shows the need both for understanding the implications of disclaiming future interests and for proper drafting. By specifically providing how property passes in the event of disclaimer, statutory problems such as this one can be avoided.

7. 1999 Disclaimer Act § 6 (Amended 2002).

2. Acceleration of Remaining Interests

A different problem arises when the income beneficiary of a trust disclaims that income interest. Applying the relation-back doctrine, the disclaimant is deemed to have died before the trust is created. For example, if parent creates a testamentary trust giving child a life income interest with the remainder to the child's children, and the child disclaims her income interest, she is deemed to have predeceased the parent on whose death the trust is created. In that event, the trust probably terminates, and the trust property passes to the child's children. However, if the disclaimant had more children after the date the trust should have been created, those after-born children would have been entitled to trust property had the disclaimer not been made. It could be argued that the trust should not terminate after the disclaimer, but instead should continue for the disclaimant's life, to ensure that all beneficiaries receive property they are entitled to.

This problem of acceleration or non-acceleration has been solved in some jurisdictions by statute. For example, the Comments to Section 6 of the 1999 Disclaimer Act demonstrate that that section

> makes a disclaimer of an interest in property effective as of the time the instrument creating the interest becomes irrevocable or at the decedent's death if the interest is created by intestate succession. A will and a revocable trust are irrevocable at the testator's or settlor's death. Inter vivos trusts may also be irrevocable at their creation or may become irrevocable before the settlor's death. A beneficiary designation is also irrevocable at death, unless it is made irrevocable at an earlier time. [Section 6] continues the provision of Uniform Acts on this subject, but with different wording. Previous Acts have stated that the disclaimer "relates back" to some time before the disclaimed interest was created. The relation back doctrine gives effect to the special nature of the disclaimer as a refusal to accept. Because the disclaimer "relates back," the disclaimant is regarded as never having had an interest in the disclaimed property.

The Comments also state that "[u]pon the disclaimer of a preceding interest, a future interest held by a person other than the disclaimant takes effect as if the disclaimant had died or ceased to exist immediately before the time of distribution, but a future interest held by the disclaimant is not accelerated in possession or enjoyment."[8] The effect of this provision is illustrated by two examples in the Comments:

> Example 5(a). Father's will creates a testamentary trust to pay income to his son S for his life, and on his death to pay the remainder to S's then living descendants, by right of representation. If S disclaims his life income interest in the trusts, he will be deemed to have died immediately before Father's death. The disclaimed interest, S's income interest, came into possession and enjoyment at Father's death as would any present interest created by a will . . ., therefore, the time of distribution is Father's death. If the income beneficiary of a testamentary trust does not survive the testator, the income interest is not created and the next interest in the trust takes effect. Since the next interest in Father's trust is the remainder in S's descendants, the trust property will pass to S's descendants who survive Father by representation. It is immaterial under the statute that the actual situation at S's death might be different descendants entitled to the remainder.
>
> Example 5(b). Mother's will creates a testamentary trust to pay the income to her daughter D until she reaches age thirty-five at which time the trust is to terminate and the trust property is to be distributed in equal shares to D and her three siblings. D disclaims her income interest. The remainder interests in her three siblings accelerate and they each receive one-fourth of the trust property. D's remainder interest does not accelerate, however, and she must wait until she is thirty-five to receive her one-fourth of the trust property.

8. Uniform Disclaimer of Property Interests Act 1999 § 6(b)(4) (West 2004).

In specific state examples, California Law states that, unless the creator of the interest provides otherwise, a disclaimed future interest passes "as if the disclaimant had died before the event determining that the taker of the interest had become finally ascertained and the taker's interest indefeasibly vested."[9] The Comments to this provision state that it "makes clear that a disclaimer has the effect of accelerating the possession and enjoyment of subsequent interests." Note, however, that it does not address the acceleration of the disclaimant's own interest, as described in the preceding example. Texas law states that a disclaimer of a future interest "takes effect as if the disclaiming beneficiary had predeceased the decedent,"[10] with the same effect as the provision in California law.

Finally, New York law states that, unless the creator of a disclaimed interest provides otherwise, the disclaimed future interest passes "as though the renouncing person had died at the time of filing or just prior to its becoming an estate in possession, whichever is earlier in time, and shall have the effect of accelerating the possession and enjoyment of subsequent interests, but shall have no effect upon the vesting of a future estate which by the terms of the disposition is limited upon a preceding estate other than the renounced interest."[11] The New York statute also provides greater detail than either the California or Texas statutes; if "there would occur a per stirpes disposition of the renounced interest or a disposition or distribution of the renounced interest by representation, then . . . the renouncing person shall be treated as having died on the same day as, but immediately after, the creator or decedent, or, if the renounced interest is a future estate, as having died on the same day as, but immediately after, its becoming an estate in possession or, if the time of filing is earlier in time, on the same date as, but immediately after, such filing." Finally, the renunciation is retroactive to the creation of the disposition.[12] The New York statute also deals with a person who holds a present and

9. CAL. PROB. CODE § 282 (West 2011).
10. TEX. PROB. CODE § 37A (Vernon's 2011).
11. N.Y. CLS EPTL § 2-1.11(e) (McKinney's 2011).
12. *Id.*

a future interest property; if such a person renounces the present interest in whole or in part, that person "shall be deemed to have renounced the future interest to the same extent."[13]

These statutory fixes cannot completely eliminate litigation, however. A South Carolina case[14] involved a mother whose will created a trust for each of her two sons as income beneficiaries with the remainder passing to her grandchildren. All of her grandchildren were children of the disclaimant; the disclaimant's brother had none. The South Carolina disclaimer statute provided for acceleration of interests, unless the will or other dispositive instrument provided for a different disposition in the event of a disclaimer. The South Carolina Supreme Court found that, because the mother's will did not contain another disposition in the event of disclaimer, the disclaimer accelerated her children's interests and the disclaimed trust property passed to them.

In a New York case,[15] a decedent created a testamentary payable on death (POD) trust for the current benefit of his son and the son's issue, with the remainder payable to the son's issue. When the testator died, the son, who disclaimed his interest in the trust, had no issue. The decedent's executors sought a ruling that the trust should continue for the son's life, rather than the trust interests accelerating and the trust terminating. However, the court disagreed, holding that the remainder interests were accelerated and passed to trusts for the decedent's other children. As a result, if the disclaimant had any children in the future, those children would never receive an interest in the trust property. As one commentator points out, this rule of acceleration is now the "default" rule for most courts.[16]

Notwithstanding this general acceleration rule, two Georgia cases[17] provide that acceleration can be defeated by the instrument creating the disclaimed interest when the remainder inter-

13. *Id.*

14. Pate v. Ford, 76 S.E.2d 775 (S.C. 1989).

15. *In re* Est. of Gilbert, 592 N.Y.S.2d 224 (1992).

16. La Piana, *Some Property Law Issues in the Law of Disclaimers*, 38 REAL PROP., PROB. & TRUST J. 207, 221 (2003).

17. Wetherbee v. First State Bank & Trust Co., 466 S.E.2d 835 (Ga. 1996); Linkous v. Candler, 508 S.E.2d 657 (Ga. 1998).

ests are contingent upon surviving the disclaimant. In one of these cases,[18] a decedent's will provided for a residuary trust for the lifetime benefit of his wife; that trust passed into further trusts upon her death for each of his sons for support and maintenance during their lifetime. If either son predeceased his mother, then upon the mother's death, or upon the son's death if he survived his mother, his interest passed to his then "surviving unmarried wife and . . . his then surviving descendants." After the decedent's death and before divorcing their respective spouses, both sons renounced their interests, seeking an acceleration of the trust interests so that the decedent's ex-daughter-in-laws and grandchildren were entitled to the trust property.

The court noted that acceleration of remainder interests occurs under the statute only when the testator does not indicate a contrary intent. Such an intent is indicated if the testator has provided that the holder of the future interest must survive the holder of the renounced interest. Here, the decedent intended that the sons' wives and descendants must survive the sons in order to take. Accordingly, the remainder interests would become "indefeasibly vested" only upon the death of the sons, and the income otherwise payable to the sons could not be distributed but rather would have to be accumulated until the sons' deaths determined who the appropriate beneficiaries would be.

Although one might argue that the acceleration of future interests ought not to be allowed because it would allow disclaimants to manipulate the result of a disclaimer, if that were the general rule, many disclaimers would be rendered impracticable because the administration would be left open until some future event. Therefore, acceleration following a disclaimer, even if it can sometimes create harsh results,[19] is a better result than non-acceleration.

3. Disclaimers Going to the Wrong Person

It is common for a disclaimant to stop short of executing all necessary disclaimers. When this happens, the disclaimer does not

18. *See* Wetherbee, 466 S.E.2d 835.
19. *See, e.g.*, La Piana, *supra* note 16, at 220-225.

accomplish its intended purpose; the disclaimed property ends up in the wrong hands (including, at times, the disclaimant's own). For example, in one situation[20] the disclaimant, after disclaiming her interest in shares of closely held stock passing under her mother's will, failed to take the additional step of disclaiming her intestate interest in those shares. As a result, the disclaimant merely caused the property to pass to herself under the laws of intestacy under state law. To make matters worse, because the executor thought the disclaimer accomplished its purpose, the executor distributed the shares to the disclaimant's children, which the IRS National Office advised amounted to a taxable gift from the disclaimant to her children.

Another example of a disclaimer that did not go far enough is set forth in PLR 200846003, under which the decedent's children were named beneficiaries of the decedent's independent retirement account (IRA). They attempted to disclaim so that it would pass through a testamentary QTIP trust for the surviving spouse. Unfortunately, after the surviving spouse died, the property of the QTIP trust was to pass to a second trust and then to the children. Because they did not disclaim their interests in this second trust, the children did not disclaim their entire interest in property. The disclaimers were therefore not qualified, and the children made taxable gifts into the trust, which in turn meant that the property came from the children, not the predeceased spouse; thus, no estate tax marital deduction was available

Disclaimants also have been known, after disclaiming into a trust, to fail to disclaim their interests in the trust itself. Because one of the disclaimer requirements is that the disclaimed property must pass to the spouse or someone other than the disclaimant, if the disclaimant is not the spouse, the disclaimer is not qualified.[21] In PLR 8617065, the husband's will left specific bequests to his children and the residue to a QTIP trust for the benefit of his wife, with remainder to his then-living descendants. The husband's descendants who survived him—two adult children and two minor grandchildren (by their guardians)—proposed to disclaim an amount of

20. TAM 9417002.
21. § 2518(b)(4)(B).

their bequest in excess of $400,000 (the credit shelter amount at the time). The disclaimants were trying to divide the interests on a temporal basis and disclaim only an income interest. Because the disclaimed property passed to a trust of which the disclaimants were remainder beneficiaries, the disclaimers were not qualified. The fact that the disclaimants' remainder interests were deemed to pass from the wife under Section 2044, because the fiduciary elected QTIP treatment for the trust, was irrelevant.[22] The proper way to have handled this proposal might have been for the wife, children, and guardian for the grandchildren to have disclaimed, with second-tier disclaimers by the children and on behalf of the grandchildren of their resulting intestate interest. This approach might have terminated the trust and increased the marital deduction, but it also would have denied the children and grandchildren who survived the wife the security of the trust's remainder interest.

In another example of failing to make multilevel disclaimers, *Hunt v. U.S.*[23] concerned the estate of a husband who died intestate, survived by his wife, 4 children, 17 grandchildren (5 of which were the children his son who predeceased him), and 10 great-grandchildren. His intestate beneficiaries were his four living children and the five children of the deceased son; the surviving spouse received a share only if there were no surviving descendants. The nine heirs disclaimed their interests, believing that all of the decedent's property would then pass to his wife and qualify for the marital deduction.

Although the disclaimants argued that the nondisclaiming grandchildren and great-grandchildren as lineal descendants could inherit only through their relationship with their parents, and that therefore their parents' disclaimers cut off any claims they had, the court held that the nondisclaiming descendants did *not* inherit through their parents, but in their own right as descendants of the decedent. Therefore, the disclaimers did not pass property to the widow.

22. Regs. § 25.2518-2(c)(3).
23. 566 F. Supp. 356 (E.D. Ark. 1983).

In *Radel Est. v. Comr.*,[24] another husband died intestate, survived by his wife and their three adult children (but apparently no grandchildren this time). At his death, he owned 115 acres of farmland worth $210,000; of that sum, $158,400 was attributable to the couple's homestead. Minnesota intestacy law gave the surviving spouse a life estate in the homestead property, with remainder to the children. The remaining intestate property passed one-third to the spouse, two-thirds to the children. To obtain a one-third outright interest in the property, the wife disclaimed her homestead interest. She argued that, as a result of her disclaimer, she was deemed to have predeceased her husband with respect to the homestead, which then passed as intestate property. However, the tax court ruled instead that the wife's waiver "caused an acceleration of the children's interest from a remainder to a fee simple absolute." Had the wife and adult children instead disclaimed their entire collective interest in the homestead property, it would have been converted to intestate property, and the wife would have achieved the result she sought.

C. Denial of Judicial Approval

Judicial approval of a fiduciary's or beneficiary's disclaimer is not automatic. For instance, a guardian often is appointed for minor grandchildren as part of a plan to redirect assets back up to grandparents. Following a disclaimer by the parents, the guardian disclaims on behalf of the minor grandchildren the interests that they would otherwise receive from that parental disclaimer. As a result, with both children and grandchildren disclaiming, the disclaimed interest passes to the grandparents. In that situation, the minor grandchildren will have lost nothing by their disclaimer. Nonetheless, some courts have not consented to the guardian's disclaimer.[25] Further, in a case in which a mother and her adult daughter died in short succession—the daughter died three months after the mother died—the executor of the daughter's estate was not

24. 88 T.C. 1143 (1987).
25. Horowitz Est., 220 N.J. Super. 300, 531 A.2d 1364 (1987).

permitted to disclaim the daughter's interest in the mother's estate, which would have resulted in the interest passing directly to the daughter's adult child undiminished by death taxes on the daughter's estate.[26]

In a California case, a testator's will was witnessed by three people: Evelyn, Marie, and Bob. The will gave Evelyn a $100 bequest and gave real property to Marie. A California statute voided a gift to a subscribing witness unless there were two other disinterested subscribing witnesses. Evelyn disclaimed her bequest and claimed therefore to be a disinterested witness, in order to permit the devise to Marie to be effective. The court refused to apply the relation-back concept, although the statute stated that "in every case, the disclaimer shall relate back for all purposes to the date of the creation of the interest." Holding that Evelyn was not a disinterested witness when she signed the will and that, therefore, her disclaimer was a nullity because she had no interest to disclaim, the court also held the gift to Marie to be void.[27]

D. When a Predeceased Disclaimant Is Not Predeceased

Even though a disclaimant is treated as having predeceased the testator for the purpose of having the disclaimed interest bypass the disclaimant, nonetheless, for other purposes, the same disclaimant may be deemed not to have predeceased the testator. A childless uncle disclaimed his share in his deceased sister's estate with the intent that the disclaimed property should pass equally to his niece and nephews, but found out after the fact the one niece (the child of the disclaimant's deceased brother A) took half the disclaimed property, and the five nephews (children of the disclaimant's deceased brother B) took only one-tenth each. This result occurs because, although the disclaiming brother is deemed to have predeceased the sister for purposes of having the

26. *In re* Morgan Est., 411 N.E.2d 213 (Ill. 1980).
27. Parsons Est., 103 Cal. App. 3d 384, 163 Cal. Rptr. 70 (1980).

disclaimed property not pass to him, he is not deemed to have predeceased her for purposes of determining that a per stirpital division must be made at his level (because he actually is alive) rather than the per capita distribution at the level of the nieces and nephews that he sought.[28]

This issue arises in other contexts as well as in the per stirpital distribution case described above. Where the testator's daughter disclaimed in order to benefit the charitable beneficiaries of the testator's residuary estate, those who would be the testator's intestate takers if the daughter had not survived claimed that they should have received notice of probate of the will and distribution of the assets and that they now had standing to contest the will because the daughter was presumed, by the disclaimer statute, to have predeceased the testator. Their claim was rejected.[29]

E. The Problem of Acceptance for State Law Purposes

One question that often turns on state law is whether a would-be disclaimant has accepted benefits from the property to be disclaimed, thus barring the ability to disclaim. This is related to, but slightly different from, the "acceptance" rulings discussed in the Section 2518 context, already discussed. Rather, these acceptance cases may affect the effectiveness of a disclaimer solely from a state law perspective (for example, if the disclaimer is made to avoid creditors).

Several decisions have found that a disclaimant had accepted benefits from property and therefore could not disclaim it. For example, in a Utah decision,[30] a garnishee attempted to disclaim an interest in trust created by his mother and avoid garnishment. Shortly after his mother's death, the garnishee met with his sib-

28. Welder v. Hitchcock, 617 S.W.2d 294 (Tex. App. 1981). *See* McGovern, Kurtz, & Rein, Wills, Trusts & Estates 84 (1988). *See* Uniform Probate Code Official 1990 Text § 2-801(d).

29. Estes Est., *In re*, 239 Kan. 192, 718 P.2d 298 (1986).

30. Whitney v. Faulkner, 2004 U.T. 52; 95 P.3d 270 (2004).

lings and divided the decedent's personal property. Thereafter, he executed a written disclaimer under which he purported to renounce his entire interest in his mother's estate. Because he accepted the personal property, property he purported to disclaim, his entire disclaimer was ineffective. The court pointed out that

> [h]ad he not accepted any property from the trust, or had he used language of partial disclaimer as he now urges he intended, [the garnishee's] disclaimer would have been effective.[31]

The garnishee's "substantial compliance" argument was not taken seriously by the court, because it was unsupported by the language and policy of the disclaimer statute. His disclaimer "was ineffective as a total disclaimer because he accepted property from the trust, and as a partial disclaimer because it did not accurately describe the interest to be disclaimed."[32]

In a South Carolina case,[33] a decedent's daughter was left a life estate in the decedent's residence with the remainder passing to the daughter's children. She took several steps that indicated acceptance: as a coexecutor, she executed a deed to the property to herself; she filed a receipt for the property with the probate court; she obtained an insurance policy in her name as property owner; and she listed the property for sale. After taking all those steps, she executed a disclaimer of her interest in the property, in which she attempted to make a qualified disclaimer. Her siblings instituted a probate court proceeding to have her children's interest in the property declared to be contingent, not vested, and to have the disclaimer declared invalid. The court found that, as a result of all of her activities with respect to the property, she had exercised dominion and control over the property and therefore could not disclaim it.

31. *Id.* at 273.
32. *Id.* at 274.
33. Hall v. Hayes, 318 S.C. 188; 456 S.E.2d 439 (1995).

Further, a Washington case[34] found acceptance of a joint bank account, which therefore barred its disclaimer (coincidentally, it relieved the would-be disclaimant's lawyer from liability for failing to advise her about the possibility of a disclaimer). Before husband's death, he owned an investment account jointly with his wife. After he died, the wife sent a letter to her financial consultant, asking him to change title to the account from both their names to her name only. The wife directed significant activity in the account after that time. Shortly after the husband's death, the wife died as well. The lawyer did not discover the joint account's existence until after the nine-month date within which a disclaimer could have been made under state law. However, the court ruled that the wife had accepted the husband's half of the joint account by changing title and directing investments; as a result, even if the lawyer knew of its existence, he could not have advised wife to disclaim it. The court determined that acceptance had occurred because the wife instructed the financial consultant to transfer the account into her own name, she ordered substantial sales and purchases within the account, and she deposited $50,000 of her own assets into the account after her husband's death.

However, in other cases courts have not found acceptance and thus have ruled disclaimers to be effective. This is especially true when the "acceptance" was simply a loan from the assets to be disclaimed. The New York Supreme Court[35] addressed the situation of a son who killed his father and the son's live-in girlfriend and then attempted to renounce his share of his father's estate. The court found that the son's late renunciation was not barred by the acceptance by his guardian of funds from the father's profit-sharing plan for criminal defense costs, because the estate and the plan were separate assets, and acceptance of one did not bar a renunciation of the other. Further, advances from the estate for the son's criminal defense costs made while the son was still a minor and before a legal guardian was appointed were the result of an informal decision among the estate beneficiaries (in which the son did not participate) and did not amount to an acceptance by the son.

---

34. Leipham v. Adams, 77 Wn. App. 827; 894 P.2d 576 (1995).
35. *In re Gates*, 189 A.D.2d 427; 596 N.Y.S.2d 194 (1993).

Additionally, a Georgia case[36] found that loans made to a disclaimant (the decedent's granddaughter) for funeral clothes that were paid back to the estate did not amount to acceptance of estate assets, and therefore the disclaimant's renunciation of her interest in the estate was valid.

F. Conflict of Laws Issues

If a surviving spouse disclaims his interest under the deceased spouse's will, does it govern real property in another state? At least one court, holding that its intestate laws cannot affect the disposition of that real property, held that its disclaimer law cannot either.[37] A different question is what law applies when a second decedent dies shortly after the death of the first decedent and both lived in different states. If the executor of the second decedent's estate wanted to disclaim that estate's interest in the estate of the first decedent, one might assume that the law of the state of the executor's appointment governs. However, the IRS has ruled otherwise.[38]

G. Undue Influence

Even otherwise valid disclaimers can be challenged on the basis of undue influence or fraudulent inducement. Such challenges are difficult to make to one's own disclaimers, however; in a case where there was a wide discrepancy in the amounts of lifetime gifts a mother made to various disclaimants, they still were unsuccessful in challenging the validity of their own disclaimers of their interests in their deceased father's estate.[39] On the other hand, heirs of an elderly disclaimant successfully challenged on the basis of undue influence of his disclaimer of jointly held property he owned

36. Jordan v. Trower, 208 Ga. App. 552; 431 S.E.2d 160 (1993).
37. Banks v. Junk, 264 So. 2d 387 (Miss. 1972).
38. PLR 7937011.
39. Schmidt v. Collins, 556 N.E.2d 933 (Ind. App. 1990).

with his deceased wife, where that disclaimer allowed the property to pass to wife's brother, who was behind the disclaimer.[40]

H. Legal Consequences of Faulty Disclaimers

Once a faulty disclaimer is made, it may not be possible to undo it. In one case, for instance,[41] a decedent died intestate, survived by his wife, two sons, and one grandchild. His sons filed disclaimers of their interests in the decedent's estate, and as a result the personal representative distributed the estate to the decedent's wife. However, the probate court later informed the personal representative that the grandchildren (the disclaimants' children) may be entitled to a portion of the estate as a result of the disclaimers. The sons then executed a "Revocation and Withdrawal of Disclaimer," which stated that the sons' intent in disclaiming was to allow their mother to be the sole heir of the estate. The court, however, held that the express language of the disclaimers was unambiguous and that the sons' interest passed by operation of state law and not by their direction. Further, the extrinsic evidence of the sons' intent in executing the disclaimer was not admissible. Therefore, their disclaimers were effective. Further, the supreme court disagreed with the sons' argument that the lower court should have applied equitable principles to set aside the disclaimers because such relief is available only where the parties acted under a mistake of fact, not a mistake of law. The sons knew the facts but not the legal effect of the disclaimers. The correct approach would have been to have guardians ad litem appointed for the grandchildren, who could have disclaimed their interests as well. This was a case of the attorney not knowing the result of the intestacy statute in South Carolina.

Disclaimers can be used to correct lawyers' errors and to prevent malpractice actions. However, if drafted carelessly or used

40. *In re* Hanzl Est., Docket No. 56358, Ohio App. (1/4/90).
41. *In re* Estate of Holden, 343 S.C. 267; 539 S.E.2d 703 (2000).

without full understanding of their consequences, or not used at all, disclaimers can also be troublesome to lawyers. For example, in an Alaska case, upon a husband's death and before his attorneys and accountants finished developing an estate plan for him, his entire $3,000,000 estate passed to his wife. The wife and three adult children sued the attorneys and accountants for $1,000,000 in damages from their alleged negligence in failing to advise wife to disclaim to save gift and estate taxes on transfers to the children. The court held that this stated a cause of action.[42]

I. The Wrong Disclaimant

A key question, when disclaimers of estate and trust assets are involved, is whether the disclaimant should be the fiduciary or the beneficiary. In TAM 8522003, a husband died three months after his wife. The husband was the sole beneficiary of the wife's estate. Wife's will was not probated; rather, the daughter (the couple's only child) filed an affidavit of heirship, stating that neither the husband (who at that point had also died) nor the daughter wanted to probate the mother's will. Subsequently, daughter as the executor of her father's estate filed an estate tax return, which excluded all of the mother's property, based on daughter's assertion that her affidavit constituted a qualified disclaimer. Although state law allowed fiduciaries to file disclaimers, the daughter filed the affidavit individually, as sole beneficiary of the father's estate. The IRS ruled that the daughter's act benefited herself only, and

---

42. Linck v. Barokas & Martin, 667 P.2d 171 (Alaska 1983). *See also* Bucquet v. Livingston, 57 Cal. App. 3d 914, 129 Cal. Rptr. 514 (1976) (Deceased husband's revocable inter vivos trust was intended to provide for marital deduction trust and for trust that would bypass estate of surviving wife. Complaint in wife's action against lawyer, who drafted the trust agreement and probated deceased husband's estate, on account of federal and state gift taxes and related costs incurred by wife because of lawyer's drafting of the bypass trust with a general power of appointment and because of lawyer's failure to advise wife to make timely disclaimer of this power, was held to state a cause of action.).

not her father's estate. Therefore, the relation-back doctrine did not apply.

Fiduciary disclaimers present a more common problem.[43] In TAM 8729002, a surviving spouse disclaimed her power as trustee to appoint trust principal to her children during her lifetime so that the trust for her benefit could qualify for QTIP treatment.[44] She did not, however, eliminate the fiduciary power to appoint, but only her ability to exercise it. Following the disclaimer, the power could still be exercised by a successor trustee. Therefore, her disclaimer was not effective to allow the trust to qualify for QTIP treatment. The correct approach would have been for all potential appointees of the fiduciary power (in this case, the disclaimant's children) in their individual capacities as beneficiaries to have disclaimed their rights to receive trust property during the surviving spouse's lifetime.

In another failed attempt to repair a QTIP trust,[45] a husband left half his estate to a marital deduction gift and the other half to a credit shelter trust, all of the income of which was distributable to the wife. The trustee also could invade principal for the support and education of descendants. The wife and children, as trustee and successor trustees, disclaimed the invasion power so that the trust could qualify for QTIP treatment. Again, however, it should have been the beneficiaries and not the trustee doing the disclaiming; because the trustee's disclaimer does not extinguish a fiduciary power, the disclaimer was ineffective to correct the trust terms. The same result occurred when a corporate trustee disclaimed its power to apply income and principal for the children's college and university education, and for the same reasons.[46]

Finally, if a disclaimant also acts as the fiduciary over assets he already has disclaimed, his fiduciary powers usually are extensive enough to violate the no-direction requirement of Section 2518(b)(4). The correct fix is probably not to disclaim those powers, but

43. *See* Rev. Rul. 90-110, 1990-2 C.B. 209.
44. TAM 8729002.
45. TAM 8505004.
46. TAM 8527009.

simply refuse to act as a fiduciary (or possibly to seek judicial approval for his resignation if he already is serving).

J. Disclaimers That Do Not Exist

Still another problem is when disclaimers do not exist, perhaps because the attorney advising the parties relies on some other technique, like judicial construction or reformation. The problem with such alternatives, under *Bosch v. Comr.*,[47] is that the IRS can ignore them.

Technical Advice Memorandum 8706014 provides a perfect example of such a problem. A husband and wife created a joint revocable trust and pour-over wills. On the first spouse's death, the trust divided into two shares, one for each of the couple's half of their community property. The surviving spouse's share remained revocable during her lifetime, while the predeceased spouse's share passed to a trust for the benefit of the surviving spouse and the couple's daughter, and that trust passed at the surviving spouse's death into two trusts, one each for the daughter and for the couple's grandchildren. Shortly before he died, the husband amended the revocable trust to redefine marital deduction gifts as referring to "the unlimited federal estate tax marital deduction, and also as expressing such amount or fractional share . . . in terms of the minimum amount which will cause the least possible amount of federal estate tax to be payable as a result of a settlor's death." Unfortunately, this amendment was irrelevant because the original trust contained no references to marital deduction gifts.

After the husband died, his share of the revocable trust was funded with $325,000 (the credit shelter amount for that year), and his remaining assets were distributed to the wife. The probate court approved this distribution in an uncontested proceeding. The IRS, however, found the probate court's distribution order was not binding for federal estate tax purposes because, under New Mexico law, "reformation of an inter vivos document will be only

47. 387 U.S. 456 (1967).

upon presentation of clear and convincing evidence of mistake." No such evidence was presented, and the IRS doubted its existence, because "the marital deduction had never figured before in Decedent's dispositive scheme." More important for our purposes, the daughter and grandchildren consented, at least by inaction, to the uncontested proceeding that whittled the size of their trusts down to $325,000, rather than disclaiming those interests. Had they instead each disclaimed their share in excess of $162,500, the trust might have been properly funded and the marital deduction obtained.

K. Failure to Disclaim Intestacy Rights

An adverse result can often stem from a qualified disclaimer if the disclaimant has an inaccurate understanding (at least in a court's opinion) of the consequences of the disclaimer. In the *Tatum* case,[48] the Fifth Circuit saved a disclaimant's estate from a significant gift tax liability that the District Court would have imposed. Here, a son disclaimed a gift in his father's will, which provided that the gift was to pass to the disclaimant's sons if he predeceased. As executor, the disclaimant obtained a court order directing the disclaimed property to pass to the disclaimant's children. Later, the disclaimant's wife died, followed by the disclaimant two years later.

The IRS issued deficiencies in both estates, claiming that the disclaimed property was a taxable transfer from both the disclaimant and his wife, because under Mississippi law, the property should have passed by intestacy to the disclaimant. The estate argued that, although Mississippi had not yet enacted the Uniform Disclaimer of Property Interest Act until after the disclaimers in question, common law required that the disclaimed property pass to the disclaimant's children. The IRS, as upheld by the District Court, argued that the language in the will that provided what would happen in the event that the disclaimant actually prede-

48. Tatum v. U.S., 106 A.F.T.R.2d 2011–5642 (5th Cir. 2011).

ceased his father was inapplicable here, because the disclaimant survived. In that event, the disclaimed property passed to the disclaimant anyway through intestacy. (Apparently the correct thing to do, in this situation, would have been to disclaim both the gift under the will and under intestacy; that didn't happen here.) The District Court reached this conclusion even though it ignored the probate court's repeated rulings. ignored a prior technical advice memorandum from the IRS itself, and acknowledged that imposing the tax was unfair.

Fortunately, the Fifth Circuit, in reaching the correct result, held first that Mississippi's anti-lapse statute applied to keep the disclaimed property out of the disclaimant's hands, and second that the testator's intent, clear from the will, was that the disclaimed property was to pass to the disclaimant's children and not to the disclaimant through intestacy.

It is disheartening that the disclaimant had to take his case all the way to the Fifth Circuit before getting the right answer. As to manifesting an intent in the document, many if not most drafters will use language substantially similar to that in *Tatum*. Nevertheless, it might be prudent in states without a uniform act to disclaim both the property itself and any rights through intestacy (unless of course the disclaimant is the surviving spouse and the goal is to take through intestacy).

L. Some Other Unintended Consequences

Finally, there can be unintended disclaimer consequences. In one case, an adult daughter disclaimed an interest in her father's estate to benefit her mother, only to find that the disclaimed interest dropped into the hands of the daughter's children.[49] In another (already discussed), a decedent's widow and children disclaimed their interests under the decedent's will but did not disclaim their

49. *See, e.g.*, Webb v. Webb, 301 S.E.2d 570 (W. Va. 1983); Ernst v. Shaw, 783 S.W.2d 400 (Ky. App. 1990); Cory v. Bryant, 149 Cal. App. 3d 323, 196 Cal. Rptr. 586 (1983). *Cf.* Tate v. Siepielski, Slip Op. No. 2-87-015-CV (Tex. App. 1987).

intestate interests. Although they thought the result would be to benefit the wife exclusively, the court found that she obtained only a right of spousal election against the will, rather than the intestate interest.[50]

M. Undoing Faulty Disclaimers

All is not lost for disclaimers that, for whatever reason, do not work as they were in intended. In the *Breakiron* case,[51] a Massachusetts District Court found that disclaimers were made in error and that therefore retroactive reformation was available, with the result that no taxable gift occurred. The written document (the disclaimer) did not reflect the intent of the parties, because there was ample evidence that the disclaimant intended to execute the disclaimer only if it did not result in a taxable gift. Even though the court found two different lines of cases, one holding that a later state law reformation of a transfer document did not affect the tax consequences of that transfer, and another holding that in the case of reformation, the original transaction remained revocable until the reformation, with the result that it was not complete for federal tax purposes. Because the IRS was a party to the action before it, the District Court followed the latter line. Even though the court granted a favorable result to the taxpayer, it also noted some courts might not be inclined to reach a similar result.

---

50. Rubinow Est. v. Comr., 75 T.C. 486 (1980), *aff'd without opin.*, 679 F.2d 873 (2d Cir. 1981).

51. Breakiron v. Guidonis, 106 A.F.T.R.2d 2010-5999 (D.C. Mass. 8/10/2010).

INDEX